Managing for Sales Results

Managing for Sales Results

A Fast-Action Guide to Finding,
Coaching, and Leading Salespeople

RON MARKS

RESULTS PUBLISHING

Warren Jamison is a professional collaborative writer. Including this one, he has written, coauthored, or edited 36 credited books, 1/3 of them issued by major publishers. More than two million copies of these books have been sold.

He has ghosted or edited at least 40 other books that do not carry his credit line. For more information go to www.warrenjamison.com or contact him at w@jamison.org.

ISBN 0-9773707-0-4

Library of Congress Control Number: 2005911004

Submit all requests for reprinting to:
Greenleaf Book Group LP
4425 Mopac South, Suite 600
Longhorn Bldg., 3rd Floor
Austin, TX 78735
(512) 891-6100

Published in the United States by Results Publishing
7010 East Acoma, Suite 201
Scottsdale, AZ 85254

www.resultsseminars. com

Composition by Greenleaf Book Group LP
Cover design by Greenleaf Book Group LP
First Edition

Printed in the United States of America
10 9 8 7 6 5 4 3 2 1

This book is dedicated to my sons, Robert Scott, Randy, and Ryan. They have taught me so much about managing and leading and have provided many examples that I have shared with audiences everywhere. They are the most important people in the world to me and I appreciate them more than words could say.
I love you guys!

CONTENTS

FOREWORD

Successfully managing salespeople in any economy is an enormously demanding job. I commend you for assuming this responsibility and for your desire to excel as a manager. The fact that you are reading this book tells me that you want not only to succeed as a manager, but also to enjoy the satisfaction of helping others grow.

It's sad but true that many people, when promoted into management, believe they have arrived and no longer need to learn. You and I know that's not the case. In my seminars, I constantly remind sales professionals that the enemy of learning is knowing. True professionals are measured by what they are willing to learn even though they think they know all there is to know. This book is a good starting point for your continued education as a sales manager. It will help you build a strong foundation on which to support the rest of your management career.

In order to manage effectively, you must develop the characteristics of a leader. Strong leaders lead by example and constantly convey to their people that the team's their daily functions areas part of a larger whole. Your role is to constantly *sell* your salespeople on selling your product *and* your company and its mission. More importantly, you must sell your salespeople on themselves and their ability to do what it takes to succeed.

Learning from the experience of others is always a good thing. I strongly suggest that you take to heart the experiences offered in this book. I first met Ron in 1979 when he joined my company as an inside salesperson. I saw a great desire in Ron for growth from the first day I met him. He did well in sales for my company and was quickly promoted to the role of seminar manager. In that capacity he traveled with me throughout the world managing our sales training seminars.

Ron was a good salesperson and representative of my company, but he really seemed to excel at leading and managing others. He was able to accomplish much with the hotel and convention center staffs to make sure our events ran smoothly. These were people he didn't know and who didn't technically work for him, and many of them whom were quite a bit older than he was. Yet, they were eager to help him achieve his desired goal for each event. What was even more impressive was that he never pressured anyone to accomplish the task at hand. The art of leading without pressure is something all managers must strive for.

When Ron started his own company in 1984, he was able to quickly build an organization of dedicated salespeople. While many companies suffer from incredible turnover, Ron's group has remained stable and consistent over the years. It has grown to become one of the most successful companies in the seminar industry.

Ron's company, like many companies, has had its highs and lows. Obviously, the highs are celebrated and relished, but the lows are really where a manager has the potential for growth. I admire Ron for his perseverance and commitment to his company, his employees, and his vendors, especially during the low points. Through strong leadership, encouragement, and positive management tactics, he has continued to build and grow his company.

We have long taught sales management skills as part of our sales training seminars. When I wanted to bring a fresh approach to dealing with the challenges in the current marketplace, I didn't look any further than my own backyard to find a flourishing sales manager. In 1999, I asked Ron to conduct the sales management portion of our training and he has been doing it quite successfully ever since.

As a practicing sales manager with both inside and outside sales forces, Ron teaches techniques that are current and pertinent to today's ever-changing business world. Salespeople are a unique breed, and to successfully manage them takes a special understanding that Ron has mastered.

Great sales managers are willing to be humble and take a backseat to the success of their people, allowing them to enjoy the limelight of achievement. As you read this book, be aware of your own ability to celebrate the success of others. When the sales professionals you manage and lead exceed your company's sales goals, your company will profit, and earning strong profits for the company is what you need to further your own career.

Read this work with an open mind. Know that these methods and techniques for managing and leading others are proven. Ron has run his company on these principles for over twenty years and through all sorts of challenges. He has been where you are today and is happy to help you achieve the success you desire for yourself tomorrow.

Tom Hopkins
The Builder of Sales Champions

ACKNOWLEDGMENTS

There are so many people who influenced me and had a significant impact on this work. My mom, Jan Waters, was the person who "sold" me on getting into sales, something I never imagined I would do. When I was just getting out of high school she got me excited about a career in selling. She also introduced me to Tom Hopkins. Tom was probably the most influential person in my business life. I started working with Tom back in 1979 and he shared so much with me that helped me to grow. Not only did he teach me from his own experience, but he introduced me to some of the most influential people in the personal development industry. My business partner, Tom Kauffman, is my good friend, and if not for him, this work would never have been completed. He has taught me much about sales management and works with me hand in hand as we apply the concepts in our own company. During my time in Oklahoma, I worked for John Shipman of Sundowner Trailers. John is an amazing leader and taught me so much about leading, vision, and the power of commitment. He gave me a tremendous opportunity to manage a larger group of people and apply many of the ideas presented in this book. I would also like to acknowledge all of the members of the Results Team, past, present, and future. I have learned much from all of the people who have worked at our group. Each of you have had an incredible impact on my life.

Managing for Sales Results

It has often been said that luck is what happens when preparation meets opportunity. I was in no way prepared for the opportunity I was afforded when I joined the Tom Hopkins sales-training organization in 1979. Since then, I have had the unique opportunity to be affiliated with the nation's leading sales trainers, I have managed my own sales team, and I have worked with hundreds of sales managers and salespeople from many diverse industries.

Sometimes one does not prepare until after the opportunity is extended. I believe this is most often the case with sales management. Unfortunately, many salespeople never receive the training they need to transition into the sales manager role. Whether you are new to sales management, thinking about sales management, or have been a sales manager for many years, *Managing for Sales Results* will assist you in improving your leadership and communication skills. When you become more prepared to lead others, your "luck" will certainly follow.

I began in the sales industry over twenty-six years ago when my mom—who was the best salesperson I had ever met prior to Tom Hopkins—persuaded me to move to Arizona where I could start a real estate career at the young age of eighteen. While going to school to get my real estate license, I worked as a telemarketer for the Hopkins organization. After a few years, I was promoted to traveling road manager and became responsible for details and logistics for seminars around the world.

In 1985, I founded Results Seminars, a company dedicated to marketing and the promotion of sales and sales-management seminars throughout the United States and Canada. We started with a staff of six and have grown the organization over the years to almost fifty employees. I clearly had no idea what I was getting into as a first-time sales manager. I figured that since I was good in sales and my customers liked me that I was a natural for sales management. Frankly, I was a failure! I struggled with staff retention, and I almost took my company to bankruptcy twice.

What I needed was instruction on how to be a sales manager. While there was an abundance of training available in the marketplace for salespeople, there was no comprehensive, technical training for sales managers. I set out to read every book I could find on the subject and discovered that few are written by people actually managing salespeople. Sure, there are good theory books on leadership written by academics, but there are few practical guides available to help managers communicate with the sales personality.

I have written this book because too many managers have never received the training they need to succeed. Managing the sales personality is by far one of the more difficult tasks in the American marketplace today. I've frequently heard managers say that they feel like they are running an adult day-care center. Remember, the salesperson has a unique behavioral style. It takes a great deal more involvement and communication to lead them to success than it does other types of employees.

In 1999 I was asked to establish and instruct sales-management courses on behalf of the Tom Hopkins organization. I had learned a great deal and had successfully built and maintained an effective sales force. I decided that as part of my development I would take a sabbatical from the training industry, and I accepted an offer to become the general sales manager of a horse trailer–manufacturing firm in Oklahoma. I moved to Oklahoma and took on the day-to-day development and management of the sales operations. We had seventy-two dealerships across the country, each with five or six salespeople; 750 employees at the manufacturing facility; and annual sales of around $62 million. I was tasked with increasing sales to $92 million within two years.

I had learned a great deal about management, especially through failures, but I had never been responsible for so many people and so much revenue. It was not going to be an easy task!

By applying the communication tactics and strategies outlined in this book, I was able to help the organization exceed its goal by reaching $98 million within the two-year time frame. Of course, in no way did I do it alone; no successful sales leader ever does. However, I can assure you that by following the strategies outlined in this text you will improve your sales force and your sales revenue will increase.

I have the good fortune to work with many companies in assisting with the training of their salespeople through our customized on-site sales and sales-management training courses. Prior to ever accepting a training assignment, I always take time in the field to get to know about the company's unique sales process. I frequently hear stories from salespeople on how badly management treats them. It is difficult to blame the managers, because they often don't know how to be effective sales managers. The greater challenge is that sales managers often believe—because they have been promoted to the executive level in their companies—that they do not need training. In most cases, they couldn't be further from the truth.

As you will learn in *Managing for Sales Results*, the abilities and skills that it takes to sell effectively will probably not be enough to efficiently lead a successful sales force. You will learn to master the critical core competencies that sales managers need to be successful in today's business environment. These include recruiting, hiring, training, motivating, monitoring, and if all else fails, firing salespeople.

How would you like to have a loyal, dedicated, and effective sales force? Managing for Sales Results will show you how, step-by-step, to lead your staff to greater sales. The strategies presented here are adaptations of proven principles and current variations on classic themes that we use each day at Results Seminars and that are used by other client companies around the world.

Leading others can be extremely frustrating. It can also be extremely rewarding. I have personally found that helping other people to grow and reach a level of success beyond their own expectations is one of the greatest feelings a leader can have. In my own experience I have seen people's income double and triple. With the subsequent lifestyle and personal development changes that come with that success, I feel as though I am making a true contribution to the world.

Ron Marks
Scottsdale, Arizona

1
SALES MANAGEMENT VERSUS SALES LEADERSHIP

Let's begin by looking at our role as the sales manager. We choose the role we play—manager or leader—through our actions. Our unconsciously made choice, largely preordained by our personality and background, will dictate our opinions and actions until we take conscious charge of the issue. Comparing the definitions of managers versus leaders suggests the following:

An effective manager understands the desired result—and coordinates the tasks and activities needed to accomplish the goal.

An effective leader inspires others with the will to accomplish the desired goal—and then provides the means for them to do it.

Let me ask you four questions:

1. Which role is more likely to develop and retain heavy hitters?
2. Which role is more likely to build a highly motivated sales force that constantly evolves into an ever-stronger team able to sustain sales in good times and bad?
3. Which role is more likely to develop its salespeople into future leading sales managers?

4. Which role is more likely to be the first to discover, and then react quickly to, new developments in the marketplace?

If your answer to any of the questions is "the manager role," your convictions may be rooted in the concept of "top-down management." Top-down calls for decision making to be reserved to managers, with little or no input from those on lower levels.

By contrast, sales leadership encourages a strong flow of information and suggestions from the bottom up, and rewards market intelligence with warm recognition.

This management concept believes in mobilizing the brainpower and market knowledge of the entire team. In order to intensify everyone's enthusiastic participation and for many other reasons, decision-making authority is passed as far down in the organization as possible. Often this calls for encouraging decision making on lower levels in the hierarchy than old-line managers are comfortable with initially.

Changing the title of their sales managers to sales leaders or *leading sales managers* is an easy first step a company can take toward creating a more flexible, creative, and productive sales force. For this innovation to have significant impact, the easy first step must be followed by more steps in the direction of encouraging the development of greater responsibility on every level. However, greater responsibility on every level cannot be effective unless it is accompanied by greater authority to make decisions.

THE FORMER-MIDDLE-MANAGER CHALLENGE

The inescapable realities of recent times have forced companies to tighten their organizations and get more production from fewer people. Slashing the ranks of middle management to the bone invariably became a significant part of the downsizing operation. This crucially affected two groups: the middle managers who left the company, and the remaining corporate executives who now had no one to delegate important tasks to.

Many former middle managers went into business for themselves. Becoming independent businesspeople meant they could no longer simply follow someone else's vision. Now they had to lead—often for the first time in their careers. Their business survival depends on how well they play this unfamiliar leadership role.

Lacking the hierarchy of large corporations, small business owners have to be managers of people as well as leaders with visionary capabilities. You have to be good at both roles. The emergence of the global marketplace has swallowed choice; now you must be a leading sales manager to prosper—even to survive. The ability to envision the future as it is most likely to impinge on your industry is also vital to your long-term growth and survival.

On the other side, with their task-oriented middle managers gone, company leaders must become good at execution in order to accomplish growth. You can be successful if you are dominant in one area and weak in the other. However, if you want to maximize your potential, you need to develop your skills, knowledge, and effectiveness in both areas—become a strong manager of people, as well as a visionary.

Leading sales managers have certain characteristics, things they do very well. See The Nine Characteristics of Leading Sales Managers later in this chapter. We have identified these strengths through trial and error, and by observation while working with many companies. On behalf of Tom Hopkins International and my own company, Results Seminars, I have worked as a corporate trainer in many companies nationwide. In these activities, I see the effects of good sales management and, sadly, what poor sales management looks like. The Nine Characteristics is an excellent checklist for managers intent on maximizing their effectiveness.

I call it a "checklist" for good reason. I fly small, single-engine aircraft. In them I've logged many hours privately and with the United States Air Force Civil Air Patrol. The take-off procedure is the same whether the aircraft is a small private plane, a commercial airliner, or Air Force One. Before pilots radio the tower for permission to taxi out to the runway for take-off, they go through a preflight safety checklist. If you ever get into a small plane and the pilot does not go through a checklist, what should you do?

Get out of that plane!

A safety checklist allows the pilot to make sure all things needed for a good flight are in order. Does a checklist guarantee a safe flight? No. Flying is not so simple. But if the pilot does *not* complete a checklist, it increases the chances of a preventable problem striking during the flight.

The pilot's checklist is a means to make sure that all pilot-controllable flight devices are functioning properly. It's the same with sales management, and for this purpose I present the following checklist for your use in analyzing your own unique mix of strengths and weaknesses.

As you go through the list, you can identify the skills and strengths you already possess, and focus on the areas where you need to change, improve, or acquire new skills.

If you fail to do these nine things well, here's my guarantee: You will suffer the multiple pains and heavy costs of excessive sales-personnel turnover. This means you'll be forced to work with an unskilled and unproductive sales force much of the time.

THE NINE CHARACTERISTICS OF LEADING SALES MANAGERS

1. Leading Sales Managers Are Dedicated to Building a Sales Team Committed to Consistent and Balanced Production

When considering checklist item one, focus on the key terms *committed* and *team.*

Committed in sales is defined as how much pain salespeople will endure before they quit. How many times they will get frustrated, rejected, and angry until they throw up their hands. Ask yourself these three questions:

What level of commitment do I have?

What level of commitment can I instill in our sales force?

Am I willing to pay the price to retain the skills and earn the respect of the salespeople who report to me?

Your answers to those questions will largely determine how far you can go in management.

Commitment is a trait we are born with. At about the ten-month mark, infants attempt to walk—a beautiful sight when it's your own child, an amusing display of poor motor skills when it's someone else's. As children learn to walk they fall, they cry, and then they pull themselves up and try again. They keep doing it until what happens? They walk. They don't look up after a fall one day and say, "Mom, the stroller might be a better option." They just keep trying until they succeed. Nothing short of walking will do. They don't know that quitting is an option.

By the time we reach adulthood, the hard knocks of life have instilled a fear of such a high level of commitment. We go along doing something we strongly want to do. Then we slam into difficulties, complications, and obstacles.

We struggle for a while like a dolphin caught in a net, and when we can't break free and swim through, we get frustrated. Bam! We can't take it anymore. Often we check out just a bit too soon, sometimes when one more effort would bring success.

As a leader, what level of commitment do I want to create in my sales force: the life-weary adult's questionable resolve, or the infant's relentless determination?

It will come down to areas such as setting goals, understanding the corporate mission, and balancing production. You don't want to rely on any one single salesperson, or even two or three, for your total production. Have you ever been in the position of relying on one or two big producers to make things happen? It's a scary place to be. It's also a place of high maintenance, because high performers typically are difficult to manage. Moreover, getting too locked-in with your top producers creates long-term growth challenges. I recall in the early days of my own company when I was struggling each month to clear payroll. I followed advice given to me at the time and put my "biggest guns on the biggest targets." Consequently I would give my best closer all of the best opportunities. It was not long before we found that he had the lion's share of our business, and I had a recruiting challenge. New team members quickly figured out that they would have to survive on the morsels that were left and began leaving the company soon after they started. I did what any bright young manager would do in that case: I decided I needed to level the playing field and took back some of the big accounts. I am sure you can guess what happened next. Yes, the top producer left the company!

What's the answer if you're in such a perilous position?

Don't take anything away from those high producers. Instead, instigate or intensify training and create incentives to inspire more of your salespeople to develop into heavy hitters. Review your territories to make sure your entire sales team has the opportunity to help create the balanced, broad-based production you're seeking.

Team. Now let's look at the other key word, *team.* Obviously we want to create a team that works well together rather than a rabble of antagonistic individuals. We want a team whose members support each other, who are ready to cover each other's shortfalls, who are not only willing to back up their fellow salespeople but are eager to do so.

I avoid phrases like "my people," because I don't own my employees. They are our team members, and they work *with* me, not *for* me. If I am successful, it is the result of the efforts of our team members. Using positive language helps create a team atmosphere. As I do work for various clients on an in-house sales or sales-management training level, one of the first things I do is listen to how management describes their team and current situation. If leaders use language other than "we," such as "them" or "I," it becomes obvious that the company has a morale challenge and probably a low level of commitment.

2. Leading Sales Managers Develop Personal Discipline, Live What They Teach, and Command Respect

Do your salespeople have to like you? No. Many sales managers are less effective than they could be because they have too great a need to be liked.

What you need as a leading sales manager—and what your salespeople need even more—is for your salespeople to respect you. Your salespeople *want* to respect you because their sense of personal security depends on it. When you ask them to do something, they need to believe it's in their best interest to do as you ask.

When James Koch founded the Boston Beer Company, soon famous for their Sam Adams beer brand, he made a commitment to spend two days a week on the trucks delivering beer in order to stay close to his customers. His company quickly became very successful. Years ago he could have hired someone to do it for him—but he still rides the beer trucks every week. Koch began this practice to stay close to his customers, but an equally valuable benefit immediately emerged—closer relationships with the salespeople driving the trucks. These relationships gave him priceless opportunities to pass on his company vision, to intensify enthusiasm and loyalty among all his employees, and to learn firsthand how the workforce felt about the company and its management. Had he elected to spend all his working time in the isolated comfort of his office, his leadership power would have been greatly reduced.

Jeff Bezos—founder and CEO of Amazon.com—regularly does his firm's equivalent of riding beer trucks. He spends several hours every month working alongside Amazon's floor employees, packing products for shipment to customers.

You have external customers, people who buy the products, and internal customers, your employees, whom you are responsible for. Many times we expend all our time and energy romancing the external customer and forget to take care of the internal customer. The natural tendency is to concentrate on trying to understand and anticipate the needs and dreams of our external customers, and to be far less concerned with the needs and dreams of our internal customers. However, if we don't equip, empower, and inspire our employees, these internal customers of ours will not take the best possible care of the external customers.

James Koch stays in close touch with his salespeople through the shared experiences of delivering the product to real customers.

Do you think knowing the boss might ride with them on any given day inspires every driver-salesperson to show up for work looking sharp? By his presence, Koch constantly elevates the levels of mutual respect and commitment to the company's vision. He also enormously increases his acquisition of vital market intelligence, which he gathers from the source.

Windshield time is crucial. Many of the things you will learn from and with your sales team behind the windshield of a car or truck will be items of commercial intelligence—some of crucial importance. Many of these items are of the sort you would never discover while holed up in your office, at least not in time to act on the intelligence before it's too late. Spend time with your salespeople in the field doing what you ask them to do. It will speak volumes for your credibility.

3. Leading Sales Managers Exercise Businesslike Detachment and Do Not Play Favorites

This is a tough one to tackle sometimes. By nature, salespeople are highly sociable extroverts. We become friendly with our sales staff. If I spend too much social time with one or a few of the team, how will the other team members perceive this? They will suspect me of playing favorites, of unevenly distributing the hot leads or best opportunities. They will harbor this suspicion regardless of whether there is the slightest truth to it. Being a leading sales manager means you never forget you're the whole team's boss and no one's particular buddy.

Your concern with inappropriate social actions should not be confined to your own behavior. An emotional or romantic relationship within the sales force is a recipe for failure. Within my company, I have had four instances (not me personally!) of managers having a romantic relationship with a member of their sales team. This renders them useless as leaders because they lose the respect of the rest of their team. I have had to terminate managers over this issue. Unless the relationship meets two tests—(1) it's in the open when the salesperson joins the team and (2) it's a marital relationship—romance between a manager and a member of the sales team is a disaster. At least I've never seen it work.

4. Leading Sales Managers Develop Future Vision and Constantly Sell "Selling" to Their Teams

Selling, selling all the time. One of our key jobs is selling sales to the salespeople. We must always look to becoming the leader, and if the sales force doesn't handle change well—and most don't—you must implement each change by selling it to the people who must now live by it. If you must make changes in things like compensation plans or territories, don't be a dictator. Instead, be a salesperson. Otherwise, you will de-motivate individuals, ignite negative energy within the group, and even lose good salespeople. Be firm but compassionate with your employees when you must make hard decisions. The new goals will not be achieved if the sales force doesn't believe in or understand them.

5. Leading Sales Managers Are Great Listeners and Attack Pending Challenges at Once

Being a focused listener is a key skill. Strong leaders must work at enhancing this vital trait. I personally struggle with this, and have to work very hard at focusing on conversations because I easily get distracted and try to multitask instead of giving an employee my full attention.

Displaying distraction is a surefire way to make a salesperson feel unrecognized or not valued. The same applies to any staff member, or even to a spouse or other member of your family.

When a meeting with a salesperson is necessary, schedule time for it. Shut off your cell phone and have your switchboard calls held. Do what it takes to eliminate or at least minimize interruptions so you can give the salesperson your full attention. These actions deliver a convincing statement: You are important to this organization.

Doing less to safeguard your meeting—whether by being inattentive or by allowing phone or other interruptions to distract you—makes a bad impression. It conveys that you do not value the salesperson with whom you are meeting. When strong salespeople don't feel valued, it becomes more likely that they will move on to other opportunities.

As a manager I learned a great way to keep my focus: shorten the amount of time it takes to get to the point and tackle the challenge. Have you ever been asked by a member of your team, "Hey, do you have a minute?" Do they ever want just a minute of your time?

So how do you encourage people to get to the point? People will talk about the weather, about the ball game, about plans after work, and because I am busy I would go into multitask mode, checking e-mail, making notes, and so on.

This often left me feeling harassed and inefficient, so in desperation, I changed my working environment. Every chair in my office was removed and a counter-style desk was built against a wall. With a plug-in laptop and a phone headset, this gave me a stand-up office environment. I became a stand-up worker.

That change of décor, which of course reflected a vast change in my personal working habits and philosophy, sent a message to the troops. The boss works standing up rather than lounging back in a leather chair; he's active, a hard charger—and he must surely admire and respect those qualities in others.

Without me saying a word, an interesting thing happened: the "Hey-got-a-minutes" suddenly became fewer and shorter—more like a minute long. The time savings and reduced frustration made the change one of the most valuable things I've ever done.

Why did this work so well?

What is the first thing employees look for when they come into your office on a hey-got-a-minute mission?

A chair.

With nary a chair in sight, something disconnects and they get to the point of the conversation very quickly. The first couple of days as a stand-up worker are fatiguing, but you'll soon get used to it. Before long, it becomes refreshing, and you have more energy, especially in the afternoon. If you have long typing projects, you may want to get a height-adjustable desk, available in any office products store. I further recommend getting one of those large exercise balls to use as a chair when working for extended periods. It does wonders for strengthening your back. I can almost guarantee something here: No one will come in and sit on the ball!

Try an experiment. Conduct a regular weekly meeting without chairs. You will be amazed at how fast the meeting will go and how quickly people will articulate what they have to say and then get on with their day.

Don't just hope challenges will fade away all by themselves. Confront them immediately and creatively. As is so frequently said but less often done: Think outside the box.

6. Leading Sales Managers Specialize in Developing People through Education and Training

Leading sales managers constantly encourage their salespeople to learn, grow, and become more skilled and knowledgeable about their business. We have been very successful at this, and have implemented numerous educational programs. Our business is selling and delivering sales training and education, so we routinely practice it in our office.

Send employees to seminars and classes; create budgets for training and tuition/admission fees. Go beyond. Attend with your employees whenever possible rather than just sending them. This is another form of windshield time, another of those priceless relationship-building opportunities. Offer training in all areas, not just in sales, because doing so creates more valuable workers.

Several years ago we implemented an automated sales force, a huge change for our company. We went from a paper system to a computerized system, in which all our salespeople synchronize schedules and contacts with laptops, thus eliminating a lot of paper. This demanded a huge mind-set change and tons of training. We had to really work at it, but now the people with us are more valuable, more productive in their work. If they choose to move on, they will have those skills on their résumés.

You may ask why you would want to improve your employees' value on the open market. As many companies do, we have two groups of salespeople, inside sales and outside representatives. The members of the inside sales team all live near our company's home office in Scottsdale; the outside representatives change base from one city to another.

Many years ago we realized the outside representatives typically stay only two or three years. They do the job well, but after a few years they're tired of basing in a new city about every eight weeks and are ready to settle in one place. To meet this challenge, we developed a "come grow and go" philosophy. When they come we encourage them to grow. When they go they will be more skilled and hence more valuable than when they came to us. On leaving, they discover their time with Results Seminars and Tom Hopkins was a positive and enriching experience. The education they gained makes them more valuable while they are with the company and they take it with them when they move on.

This philosophy also benefits the company. It instills a higher level of commitment to our company's vision in our entire staff, and much referral business comes our way through former employees. When I began as a sales manager, I remember being taught by Tom Hopkins that I would need to help my salespeople to be as great as I am—almost. Obviously this means they must think I am pretty great!

The word *almost* bothered me. If some of my salespeople thought they were "greater" than me, they would want to be promoted or take over my company. Yet *almost* sounded as though I was being told to hold them back.

As I have grown as a manager, I have realized the real meaning: The person who has to continue to grow is me! With a rapidly changing environment, I have had to be at the forefront of technology; I have had to constantly grow and stay ahead, not hold my team back.

7. Leading Sales Managers Look at Change as Healthy and Promote Risk Taking

Change gives us two choices: We can embrace it or fight it. We can move forward with new concepts, or we can stagnate with no-longer-the-most-efficient methods. Every time we opt for the second choice, we put a brake on our growth, profitability, and survivability. To make this welcoming-change concept work, you need to convince your team of another fundamental and far-reaching concept: It's okay to fail. You have to reinforce the proposition of this really being your attitude by praising rather than condemning failure. Unless you do, your team won't try anything new. Getting behind this concept means you choose the dynamic response to challenges and change rather than a static do-nothing response that guarantees being swept aside by change.

When you implement a change of some kind, remember there is pain in change for employees, as discussed in Characteristic 4. Be sensitive to this.

8. Leading Sales Managers Praise in Public and Criticize in Private

Although it's plain common sense, many managers fail at this characteristic. My first exposure to this concept came from reading Dr. Kenneth Blanchard's *The One Minute Manager*. One of the management concepts he popularized in the book is that if you have something positive to say about an employee, round up everyone you can find and share the news. But if it's something negative, keep it private between yourself and the employee. Avoid having anyone else present during a negative interview.

Key personnel who need to know about it can be informed later. Extra witnesses increase the employee's embarrassment, humiliation, and resentment, and some of this will spill over to other members of the staff. Don't talk around the water cooler about the issue either.

Most of us know this as a general rule, but when I didn't do it one time, I got a good wake-up call to follow this maxim without exception. I rode along with Bob, one of our top sales performers, and two people who were just joining our firm. I had asked Bob to do some coaching and wanted them to see a professional presentation.

"Hey Ron, how do you think I did today?" Bob asked at dinner. What was Bob looking for? Some praise in front of the new field guys.

"Hey, you're great, you're the best, but you got a little 'speaker fever,' buddy," I responded.

In our business, speaker fever is the kiss of death. Too much of it means you are convoluting the message so it loses its value, perhaps by sharing excessive amounts of the old "me, me, me." Maybe you have seen this. You train some brand-new team members in a specific presentation and give them the tools they need. Six months later you ride along with one of them to observe and you wonder, where did this presentation come from? It's so full of stories that you get confused—and you know what you're selling! This is speaker fever. Well, the new people were aware of this. The subject was dropped and we went on with dinner. But the next morning, Bob pulled me aside.

"You know Ron, I really work hard for you. I'm one of your top guys. You made me look pretty foolish last night, and I don't appreciate it."

I thought about it, and agreed with him. I told him I appreciated his honesty. The praise of his strengths should have been shared with the group; the speaker-fever issue should have been discussed in private. It may also have been appropriate to discuss speaker fever as a topic with the new salespeople separately.

You have to be aware of how random remarks are perceived as well. In a sales meeting, have you ever poked fun, cracked a joke, or tried to make light of something instead of dealing with the issue straight on? If your jollity is geared toward a specific individual, he or she will feel picked on in front of the others.

Bottom line: If you have something good to say, fill the conference room with members of your team and ladle out the praise. The benefits are huge and fall into two slots:

1. The individuals receiving the public recognition are inspired to do even better, and their feelings of loyalty and dedication are intensified.

2. Everyone hearing the public praise sees that praiseworthy action is recognized.

However, if what needs to be said is controversial or in any way negative, it needs to be said in a one-on-one situation.

9. Leading Sales Managers Enjoy the Success of Others and Take Responsibility for Outcomes

You were pretty successful in sales before being promoted to management, right? Most companies get their sales-management personnel from their sales force.

Many times companies promote a top performer out of sales and into management. The reasoning is that a top performer knows how it's done and can best re-create his or her performance in others. However, unless the promoted top performers are given excellent training and orientation in their new responsibilities, their chances of doing well in sales management are less than fifty-fifty. Most people who fail in management don't feel positive about going back to sales with the same company, so they move on. Imagine if a leading NBA basketball team had a policy of taking the leading scorer off the court each year and promoting him to coach. How long do you think such a team would continue to be a leading team? You're right, not very long!

Consider carefully before promoting top performers to management. They must have a strong desire and aptitude for the promotion; it must pay better; and you must be prepared to give the manager candidates the best possible training. Otherwise, you'll probably lose a top performer without gaining a leading sales manager.

Think about your top producers. When a sale is made, who gets the credit for the success? The salesperson. But when a transaction goes south, whose fault is it? The lead's, the prospect's, the company's, but not the salesperson's. Basically, salespeople accept the credit for success and delegate the debit for failure. Even on easy sales, in which the customers almost beg you to take their money, salespeople will step up and take the credit.

How long would a top leader last if he always stepped up and said, "*I* turned this division around, *I* did this, *I* did that"? Not very long. A good leader must delegate success and accept failure—the opposite of what good salespeople do. Many of us are not good at this. If you are really challenged by this idea, you may have more success staying in the sales side of the business, which is okay. But getting excited about other people's success is a genuine leadership quality.

All sales managers have a favorite success story they love to tell about an employee they helped mold into a more successful individual. One of my favorites is about John. I first met John as the potato chip guy who came around every week to fill up the vending machine at the office. He was a great guy; everybody loved him. We got to know John and talked him into joining our firm.

I don't know what John made pushing potato chips, maybe $26,000 a year. I do know that with training, guidance, and encouragement, John ended up earning from $120,000 to $130,000 a year with us. Wow! We took someone who thought $26K is as good as it gets, and developed his skills and strengths until he achieved a six-figure level of success. Isn't that cool?

Those are the nine characteristics. For some of them, you may think, "Yeah, yeah, been there, done that, got the T-shirt." Others may hit a nerve. Look at all nine as a unit. If you don't do these nine things well, what are the results, the costs? Look behind you. If no one is following, it's a pretty good clue you are not leading well. Get your house in order before you start working on everyone else.

If you really want to make a career based on leadership, one of the things you can and probably should do is to look outside your business for ways to practice and enhance the skills and competencies it takes to lead people. Go into your community and lead a group of volunteers. Reaching a leadership position in volunteer groups is almost always very easy—just volunteer to do the unpaid work. Want to spend more time with the family? Volunteer for an organization your family is active in, and do two things at once—spend more time with the family and boost your leadership skills.

Traditional management gives you carrots and sticks. The sticks are the "or else's" and the carrots are the incentives. Whether the venue is your child's soccer team, your house of worship, or your community, when you manage volunteers you generally work with your peers. This means you have lost the sticks and you don't have a whole lot of carrots. To motivate and enlist the willing cooperation of volunteers, you have to use public praise, recognition, and achievement awards. You need to delegate as much responsibility as possible, not so much to escape doing the work yourself as to encourage participation and provide credibility for praise and recognition.

Volunteer leadership will sharpen your communication skills because it demands sensitive tact and thoughtful diplomacy in all your contacts with the peer-volunteers you're leading. In other words, you'll need all the things you know you should use at the office but somehow don't.

When managing an activity for children, such as Little League, which I have done for my three sons over the years, it's not always about the kids; it's more about the biggest challenge: managing the parents.

However, if you can get good at volunteer leadership, when you go back to the workplace and get the stick and carrot back, you won't have to use them as much—which means you'll get more production for the peso.

Learning, practicing, and perfecting new leadership tools in arenas where no costly business mistakes can be made will increase your value as a leading sales manager. It also signals you are ready to take on greater responsibilities.

For example, if you are right-handed and you break your right arm, you are going to have to get really good at utilizing your left hand for simple tasks like brushing your teeth or using your cell phone. When you regain the use of your right hand, you'll be somewhat ambidextrous and have more tools to work with. If you're serious about becoming the best leader you can be, volunteer to manage volunteers.

This is also excellent advice if you are an executive manager responsible for grooming and promoting other managers. Before you give them the management assignment, ask them to take on the project of leading other volunteers. Make it a part of their apprenticeship program.

What is the cost of *not* performing the nine characteristics effectively? Weak leadership causes rapid, out-of-control turnover of your sales team. Turnover of salespeople can be good when management controls it, but when people are leaving before you are ready and perhaps even taking other valuable people with them, it becomes a challenge.

One of the great tests of leadership is to simply look behind you. If no one is following, then you have a pretty good clue that your leadership skills need work.

THE COST OF SALES TEAM TURNOVER

In many countries the word *turnover* actually has positive connotations as it represents the amount of revenue a company generates on an annual basis. In the retail world it can be the number of times you sell through your inventory. In most companies, however, *turnover* has negative meaning as it refers to people leaving your company, mostly prematurely. There are many "costs" to salesperson turnover. Disrupted relationships with clients and the negative impact on employee morale are two of them. The biggest cost, though, seems to be the money you invest in hiring new sales people. This cost can generally be measured in three categories.

1. Cost of Acquisition

Acquisition cost begins with the advertising expense to bring candidates in for interviews, whether it's via print, radio, or the Internet. Added to that is the cost of conducting the interviews, calculated in terms of the value of the interviewer's time, plus the cost in managerial time or outsourced checkers to run whatever background checks and verifications of résumé claims are required by company policy. Thus acquisition includes all the costs associated with getting to the point where you reach your hand across the table and ask the person to join the team.

2. Cost to Competency

The second element is the cost of taking new hires to the point where they can do the job on their own. This element includes training, any start-up salary paid during the training period, licensing, travel expenses—anything required to bring them to the company's standard of competency.

3. Intangible Cost

This final element, and the most difficult to manage, consists of two parts: opportunity cost and emotional cost.

Opportunity cost is the loss of sales an experienced salesperson would have made but the new employee did not. Missed opportunities can be costly.

Tony, one of our management-seminar attendees, told me during a break that the opportunity cost per new hire in his company is about $40,000. In his experience, new people blow at least two sales, at $20,000 a sale, before they figure out how to do it.

So opportunity cost can be substantial but hard to determine. You can calculate opportunity cost on the gross billing amount of the lost sales, on the projected net profit loss, or on some figure in between.

Emotional cost is the trauma that bringing in a new person inflicts on the rest of your sales force. When I hire a new member, I introduce the person to the rest of the team and share my confidence in the new hire's potential in our firm. Do you think the existing employees are thinking something along these lines?

"Oh, goody, here's someone who will shoulder some of our burdens. We need all the help we can get."

Not a chance. Your sales force perceives a new team member as someone who will take another slice of the pie.

Many salespeople think finitely, not infinitely—only a certain amount of business is available, they believe, so the more people sharing it means each gets less. We say they "think finitely," but actually they don't *think* finitely about this issue—they *feel* finitely about it. In other words, they react emotionally, not rationally, to the new hire.

The emotional expense comes in when we, as managers, recruit new people into the fold, and the existing sales force starts thinking about who will get fired, or whose leads or territory will be cut. Some will think, "There aren't enough leads for me to run now, so how are they going to feed another mouth?" This causes negativity or anxiety within the sales force, and this immobilization will cost the company sales.

Take a few minutes to complete the Cost of Acquisition worksheet to help you determine what salesperson turnover could be

COST OF ACQUISITION

Your company's ballpark estimate per person hired

Classified and Internet advertising for salespeople $_____

Travel and entertainment for recruiting $_____

Hiring manager's time: _____ hours @ $_____   = $_____

Referral or agency fees $_____

Subtotal $_____

Cost to competency

Training fees: $_____

Training manager's time: _____ hours @ $_____   = $_____

Travel and entertainment for training period $_____

Start-up compensation: ___months @ $_____ $_____

Subtotal $_____

Intangible cost

Opportunity cost $_____

Emotional cost $_____

Subtotal $_____

Total of all categories per person $_____

Multiply by number of people hired per year   x__

Total annual expense for company $_____

costing your organization. You may need to get some input from the accounting team. Don't expect they will have these numbers readily available for you. Most companies put all these expenses in various places on an income statement, and it may take a little recasting of the numbers to come up with accurate estimates, let alone the exact amounts. It will be worth it however, as once you see what turnover is costing your company, you can go about the business of managing it.

Acquisition and turnover costs vary substantially from company to company. I have seen everything from $6,000 to $100,000 depending on the depth of training, signing bonuses, start-up salaries, and the cost of searching for new employee candidates.

The Employment Management Association, based in Raleigh, North Carolina, conducted a nationwide study over a six-year period that revealed an average amount of $8,512 for the cost of acquisition and the cost of competency. They did not gather information on the intangibles, the opportunity and emotional costs, because too many variables are involved.

A key question: Is the $8,512, or whatever amount you determine from this exercise, a cost or an investment? It's a cost when a new hire does not stay long enough to become productive. It's an investment when the new hire develops into a productive long-term member of your team.

Let's suppose I could give you a surefire plan guaranteed to provide salespeople who will stay with you for at least ten years, meet all sales quotas, do all the paperwork, and treat the customers well. Would you give me a check for $8,512 for each salesperson you hire under my surefire plan?

Of course you would. Unfortunately, I can't promise to do it. However, as managers we have no problem with investing that sum for someone who will stay with us. But we hate putting so much overhead and effort into people who soon turn negative, and maybe take a couple of others with them on their way out. This drives us nuts. As leaders, we must understand what this expense is so we can manage it.

How do we break it down so we can reduce it and bring it into control? How can we keep productive people for a longer term?

The answer starts with a well-thought-out selection process, followed by an effective training program. Incentives and compensation plans must provide ample motivation and a company vision the salesperson can be enthusiastic about promoting. Leading by example is a reliable way to increase the respect new hires have for their managers. Motivation also depends on mutual respect based on the salesperson's conviction of the firm's honesty and fairness, its willingness to promptly resolve grievances, its freedom from favoritism, and its lack of tolerance for inappropriate behavior in the workplace.

SUMMARY

Sales leadership, in contrast to mere sales management, encourages a steady flow of information and suggestions from the bottom up and rewards market intelligence with warm recognition. This approach harnesses the brainpower, enthusiasm, and market knowledge of the entire team.

Sales managers who lead and inspire their salespeople to consistent performance at a high level have nine characteristics:

They are totally dedicated to building an effective sales team.

They possess personal discipline.

They do not play favorites.

They constantly sell "selling" to their teams.

They are great listeners and act quickly against new challenges.

They develop their teams through education and training.

They look on change as healthy and promote risk taking.

They praise in public and criticize in private.

They enjoy the success of others and take responsibility for outcomes.

To push as much decision-making authority as is prudent to lower levels, leading sales managers must accept that mistakes will be made. Foster an environment in which people can make—and learn from—their own mistakes. The best leading sales managers determine the actual cost of hiring salespeople and work hard at controlling that expense category. They realize that by properly recruiting and hiring, they can increase profitability through cost containment.

How do you maintain the momentum and motivation of your employees?

When you look at a company and particularly at its sales management structure, you see what's called *manpower*. That term is used for simplicity's sake even though many, or sometimes all, of the salespeople are women.

Realistically, your manpower consists of ten to twelve persons who you can manage directly. If you are a good leader, very directive in your approach, you can delegate effectively and manage more people.

Contrast this to horsepower. Do you consider one horsepower to be a single horse standing in a field chomping grass? The definition of a single horsepower is one horse pulling at maximum capacity, which is sometimes further defined as being about 550 foot-pounds of work per second. If you have twelve people in your group who are your "peoplepower," do you really have twelve individuals, each pulling all the weight she or he possibly can? You probably have three to five working at full capacity. Typically about a third of your group is doing so.

Consider your current sales team. Based on our research, the average sales force under a single manager in the United States is about twelve people. These dozen sales professionals fall into four categories. Amazingly, most sales forces seem to be divided equally across these categories. I think you will find that in order to upgrade your sales team and constantly improve your peoplepower, you will need to manage these categories and help your team move through to the upper levels. In Tom Hopkins's early management training he named these four groups as follows:

Champion: Your champion salespeople are your top performers, the salespeople who know what to do. They do the job extremely well and always bring the best returns. You live for your champions, and while they are very productive, their egos will demand much of your time. You will also find they will constantly be working you for incentives, higher commission rates, and special deals.

Stable: Your stable team members are the sales professionals who know how to do the job, take great care of your customers, and create a consistent flow of sales revenue, minus the highs and lows you may experience with your champions. The stable group is very important because they are the ones who pay the bills! They are also a very frustrating group, because you always feel they could do so much more. For various reasons, however, they choose lifestyle over higher income. This is okay! You will find them to be lower maintenance and that is always a good thing.

Marginal: Your marginal group are the salespeople in no-man's-land, so to speak. They are not really good enough to keep around, yet not bad enough to fire. Many companies keep people in this category around because management lacks the full-time, proactive recruiting plan discussed later in this chapter. Since these companies lack a productive pipeline of qualified applicants or an effective recruitment program, they must keep people around who otherwise should move along. When considering these marginal sales performers, many managers feel twinges of guilt, believing they should or could have done more to help this person grow and succeed. If you have these feelings, meet them head-on. Call any such marginal people in, tell them you must see them graduate to stable status or take their talents elsewhere. Make it clear in specific terms exactly how they must improve their performance to stay, and ask whether they are willing to make the necessary effort. Be prepared to segue into a termination interview if they are unwilling to commit convincingly to a program of performance improvement.

Challenged: The last group comprises the leftover sales performers who are below par and should be allowed to pursue their goals somewhere else. That is a polite way of saying you should fire them! Since this group is always in flux, always in disarray, managers need to be persistent in helping these people move out of the company.

As I travel around the country on our management seminars, almost all sales managers tell me how long it takes them to realize where they have made a hiring mistake. This period usually is between 60 and 120 days. Yet when I ask how long the managers wait before making a termination, they say they usually wait between 180 and 240 days. The best thing you can do for salespeople who are not performing is let them move on quickly into their next career.

Once you assess your current team, you can then go about the work of upgrading your sales force. The most successful managers are always looking for new sales professionals to replace their challenged and marginal team members.

As we set up your recruiting program, it is important to note that in order to attract qualified sales professionals, you must first know what you want.

CLEARLY DEFINE WHAT YOU WANT IN A SALES PROFESSIONAL

We use a device from the Dale Carnegie Management Course, which I highly recommend, called a Position Results Description. Basically, it defines the job in results expectations versus tasks performed. It's a very neat device to help manage the results. You set up major goals and their key result areas, such as customer service, follow-through, and sales goals. Then you set a performance standard with each key result area: "This task will be satisfactorily performed when ten new accounts are established each quarter," or "when a closing ratio of 60 percent is achieved." We have found the Position Results Description is an extremely helpful device in clearly outlining the position you are looking for in sales. Shown here is an example of a position results description for a field sales representative. The concept can be extended into all roles within your organization.

By outlining the position in this manner, you can clearly express your expectations to each of your salespeople or to a sales manager. This is also an excellent device to use during your regular performance reviews, as we will discuss in a later chapter.

OUTLINE THE BEHAVIORAL STYLES YOU HAVE SEEN IN SUCCESSFUL PEOPLE

You probably already know what behavioral styles work in your business. If not, many tools are available to help you identify which types of behavioral styles will be most effective in your organization. Start by identifying these styles and determining which of them you need in your sales process.

You will need to find different types for different areas of the sales process. You may have a champion salesperson who can close

POSITION RESULTS DESCRIPTION: FIELD SALES REPRESENTATIVE

Major Goal: Sell product directly through in-field presentations and increase sales overall as described.

Key-Result Area 1: Activity

Performance Standards
My job in this area will have been satisfactorily performed when
1. 50 qualified referrals have been faxed to my inside team each week
2. 25 leads have been generated and emailed to my inside team each week

Key-Result Area 2: Productivity

Performance Standards
My job in this area will have been satisfactorily performed when
1. I have a minimum average of 40% closing ratio
2. My cancellation percentage is below 20%
3. I have a minimum average of 20 sales per month and have a minimum of a 30% upgrade ratio

Key-Result Area 3: Quality

Performance Standards
My job in this area will have been satisfactorily performed when
1. Appointment confirmation calls are made 5 business days prior to the scheduled meeting,
2. I have contacted my inside teammate if I have attempted to reach the decision maker at least three times without success
3. I have arrived 15 minutes early to each appointment and discussed with the meeting leader any areas of concern,
4. I have solidified company financial participation and the necessary details to collecting the investments at the conclusion of each meeting
5. Following each meeting, I have met with the meeting leader to get feedback and generate referrals

Key-Results Area 4: Follow-up

Performance Standards
My job in this area will have been satisfactorily performed when
1. I have provided feedback to each inside team member on the meetings I performed for them via voicemail, e-mail, or live over the phone
2. I have communicated weekly with my inside team and confirmed specific dates for collection of my pending sales.

Key-Results Area 5: Administration

Performance Standards
My job in this area will have been satisfactorily performed when
1. I am using the company client resource management (CRM) system to record all notes and input meeting results
2. My team has overnight-mailed our sales results and non-buyer data forms each Monday and Thursday
3. I respond to e-mail requests in a timely manner

Key-Results Area 6: Attitude

Performance Standards
My job in this area will have been satisfactorily performed when
1. I have avoided negativity and gossip and if necessary have enlightened my teammates to their negativity if I thought it was affecting my performance
2. Conflicts and other challenges are kept within an appropriate "need to know" circle of influence
3. I have spoken with my manager weekly to discuss my performance and the team's performance
4. I am **coachable** and I take feedback on PRD issues in a positive manner and apply it as soon as possible

a high percentage but can't properly fill out a quote for services to be rendered. Faulty quotes usually lead to one of two outcomes: (1) the company finds itself obligated to provide services in excess of those being paid for and loses money on the transaction, or (2) the company turns the job down and loses a customer. One of the most important behavioral traits we realize we need right up front is that the salesperson be computer literate. In our system and with today's technology, salespeople must know how to use a computer or they are of little use to our team. I recently had to let a very competent salesperson go because he could not get his head around the computer. He just could not make it work, and we could no longer carry his workload. Even though he was a good producer, we had to make the move. Now, when we look to attract new sales professionals, we need to know up front that they can work with technology.

Learn to identify the existing behavioral styles people possess during the selection period, and hire people with the styles you need. The Salesperson Behavioral Profile Checklist is a list of the traits that we have found to be most important for our company.

SALESPERSON BEHAVIORAL PROFILE CHECKLIST

Personal integrity and intellectual honesty
Sales skills/people skills/relationship management skills
Self-disciplined; understands self-responsibility
Sense of urgency
Good work organization
Goal oriented and motivated to earn an above-average income
Positive outlook and attitude
High self-esteem
Assertive social style
Industry, company, and product knowledge
Client market-share orientation
Team player: independent yet supportive
Effective follow-through
Continuing educational achievements
Public-speaking ability/communication skills
Generous with thanks and appreciation
Professional manner and demeanor
Computer literate

REALIZE WHAT SALESPEOPLE WANT FROM YOUR COMPANY

Just as you want hardworking, dedicated employees, your employees will have expectations of you. Face the facts: People work to support themselves, their families, and their interests. They will want things in return for their time and effort unless they are independently wealthy and work for the fun of it. To my knowledge, the only person who has done this was Jacqueline Kennedy Onassis, who became an editor at a major publisher at a nominal salary after her children were grown. She was a multimillionaire at the time.

Consider what salespeople are looking for in a compensation plan:

1. Adequate income for adequate performance, superior income for superior performance
2. Incentives for special achievement
3. A base of fixed income for security purposes
4. At least primary benefits
5. An opportunity for advancement
6. A method to measure performance
7. Equitable treatment for all sales team members; no favoritism or special deals
8. A feeling of being a valuable member of the company
9. Flexibility in the plan, sensitivity to changing conditions
10. A plan that is simple and easily understood

So in consideration of what they will want, and knowing what you want from the salesperson, you can call on a number of different options to construct a plan able to achieve nearly all of the stated objectives.

COMPENSATING YOUR SALES FORCE EFFICIENTLY

How you decide to build your company's sales compensation plan will depend greatly on what specific objectives you wish to accomplish. My goal here is to share some of the things other companies have done and what we have learned regarding paying salespeople. These suggestions will give you a foundation to help you establish a successful plan for your team with minimum error and effort.

You may not have much control over the financial compensation plan for the sales force in your company. However, you may have input, and will want to have clear, well-thought-out suggestions when compensation plans are under review. As a leader, you should have control over some of the nonsalary or intangible compensations.

There are two main objectives in the design of a sales compensation plan: (1) to reward your salespeople so their earnings will be directly related to the value of their contributions to the company, and (2) to enable your company to stimulate its sales teams to focus their efforts in directions designed to profit them while helping the business meet its sales objectives.

The two objectives are closely interrelated. Neither can safely be allowed to dominate while the other is ignored. They are mutually interdependent. To accomplish these goals, your plan should be sound, equitable, and as simple as possible.

The first step you should take in designing your compensation plan is to refine what your specific sales goals are for your business. What is it you wish to accomplish by bringing on a salesperson? Obviously you want to increase sales, but specifically by how much? How do you intend to reach the goal you are setting? What will be the salesperson's specific responsibilities—just continue to take the walk-ins, or do proactive sales work? Or are you looking to groom someone to eventually take on a new location or be promoted into management?

All those questions should be carefully considered. You must also consider how the industry, on average, pays its salespeople. My research has not found a usable national standard because it's really a local issue. Whether your plan is lucrative enough to attract and retain the right kind of qualified people in your market area will always be the key concern.

Salespeople are traditionally paid in three basic methods: Base salary is guaranteed income regardless of specific performance levels. Commission is based on the salesperson's specific performance. Many companies now also pay based on group performance, which we like to call a "team bonus."

1. *Salary.* This type of compensation is attractive to the salesperson, tough on company cash flow, not necessarily performance based, and encourages inept salespeople to stay longer. In our company, we start with a higher base salary and shift to fee-for-service as competency increases.

2. *Straight fee-for-service (commission).* This type of compensation is performance based, limits personnel resource pool, is easy on the company, and is a greater opportunity for the salesperson.

In this book, the term *fee-for-service* replaces the more common term *commission*, which has a negative connotation and is not used in the Tom Hopkins material. Fee-for-service should be used to inspire your salespeople.

3. *Override on total team performance (team bonus).* This type of compensation tends to eliminate conflict among the salespeople and create more teamwork. On the downside, it also tends to hold your top performers back and to encourage the inept to stay on longer.

By itself, a compensation plan will not motivate your salespeople to achieve their highest potential performance for themselves and the company. To accomplish that greatly desired result and make the whole process reach the highest level of effectiveness, you must engage in other leadership, counseling, and motivational activities.

We have found that a three-tier compensation system works best. By combining the elements of (1) a base salary with (2) a fee-for-service program and (3) a team bonus, we have been able to get the most from our sales team. At the same time, our three-tier compensation plan provides our sales team with the greatest opportunity for individual growth, as well as promoting company growth. In addition, we provide several levels of daily, monthly, and annual performance incentives designed by our sales manager. They are generally non-cash-based rewards.

Ideally, you will set a salary figure just high enough to give your salespeople some feeling of security and yet not be enough for them to survive on. You have to decide how much sales salary your business can afford—if any. We provide the minimum we can get away with to attract quality people, who rely heavily on performance results for higher pay. The salary you set will depend greatly on your geographic area. In 2004, we paid $750 per month, which was 15–20 percent of our salespeople's average total pay. You must also consider labor laws and regulations, as many job classifications require the employee to be paid at least the minimum wage.

Obviously, you will need to determine the actual percentage you wish to pay per unit sold. You must first decide if you wish to pay the percentage on gross sales or gross margin. It is becoming increasingly popular for companies to pay on the margin. In other words, total sales price less costs of goods sold, which includes product cost, freight, and finance charges. I highly recommend paying on margin, not gross. This is especially critical if you allow the salesperson any negotiation authority. Your salespeople see your margins under this type of plan, which many managers see as its main drawback. However, we have found that it creates more of an ownership attitude if the salesperson knows how much the company is earning on the gross level. They won't know how much you make, though, because they do not need to know how much your overhead costs are. So the net remains confidential.

If you choose to pay on the gross amount, make sure you are explicit in what the salesperson can do or not do in terms of the giveaways inherent in setting discounts and terms. I have found that when a salesperson is paid solely on the gross amount, there is no end to how generous they can be with my money.

I would further recommend paying some sort of increasing, retroactive percentage scale as higher volumes are reached. For example, on a monthly basis

0–4 units/accounts	=	20 percent of gross margin
5–9 units/accounts	=	22 percent of gross margin
10 or more units/accounts	=	25 percent of gross margin

This allows salespeople to clearly see where they can earn additional income. I look for the fee-for-service element to comprise about 70 percent of total annual income.

As you work at crafting a safe and equitable compensation system, be realistic. The typical salesperson will always find a way to sandbag a few sales and manipulate the system. Expect this, build an allowance for it into your figures, and relax. Be content to plug each hole in the system as you discover it.

The third level of regular pay is a team bonus based on total team performance over a given period. For our little company, this has been one of the best decisions I ever made. In addition to the other bases of pay we have discussed, we establish in advance a gross profit goal for a specific period. You can base the goal on anything you wish: numbers of units sold in a quarter, total volume, or gross margin. I recommend you base it on gross margin. We have found that this creates a sense of ownership among our team, allowing them to think like an owner when it comes to spending money, time, and other resources.

Make sure the goal is achievable. Don't make it too easy, of course, but not so out of reach it's perceived as a joke. I have seen companies wave an unrealistic bonus goal over their salespeople only to have the sales team laugh at it. If they take it as an insult to their intelligence, they certainly won't bother to reach for the unrealistic level.

When companies set an unreasonable goal, I'm not sure whether they hope to get the staff to really strive for it for everyone's benefit, or if they hope it creates some increase in sales volume that in the end they won't have to pay for. When a team bonus plan is set up in such a cynical manner, it strikes heavy blows against loyalty to the company and goes far to destroy respect for management. It also gives the strongest salespeople a powerful new incentive to go elsewhere.

When a team bonus plan is based on reachable goals and the team buys into the program, it's best to set it up for quarterly or biannual pay-outs instead of annual, because people lose interest in striving for the goal if the time period is too long.

The team bonus also creates a sense of accountability among other team members. We have found peers encouraging each other, holding each other accountable, and generally picking up some of our leadership responsibility. They have a stake in the outcome. It is also designed to compensate people for going above and beyond their individual responsibilities, such as taking messages for someone else, writing up a sale for another salesperson who is not on the floor, and handling a service or delivery issue for someone else's customer. It also helps smooth over those situations when a be-back does come back and is written up by another salesperson. It generally fills in areas where a few members of the team felt they got the short end of the allotment of leads or accounts, or some other specific event in the sales process.

The team bonus can also include nonsales staff. This has been a very positive program with our group. Imagine if your administrative staff—the receptionist, the accounts receivable personnel, the product supply coordinator, the lot attendant—had a direct interest in to the success of your sales team. Including them in a team bonus plan encourages them to answer the phone in their most professional manner, inspires them to respond quickly to billing issues, and motivates them to get products and supplies out fast to clients and the sales force. It defuses any lingering resentment of the "highly paid" salespeople.

If we achieve a goal, everyone gets a share of it. The team bonus creates a catch-all community feeling throughout the sales department or organization.

In the 2004 Major League Baseball World Series, the Boston Red Sox finally broke the curse and won their first championship since 1918. The MVP (most valuable player) was Red Sox left fielder Manny Ramirez. Ramirez played in virtually every inning of the postseason and contributed immensely to the Red Sox victory. Another Red Sox player, Dave Roberts, was put into the game as a pinch runner and made only one appearance during the entire postseason. Roberts stole a base and turned the tide against the Yankees in the American League play-offs.

When the World Series bonus checks were handed out to each player, how much more did Manny Ramirez receive than Dave Roberts?

The answer is nothing. They got the same bonus and each of them got one ring. Now, Manny Ramirez's fee for service each year is a great deal higher because he currently provides more value to the success of the team. But as team members, Ramirez and Roberts both provide value because baseball relies on team effort.

We have tied our team bonus to a target gross margin over a ninety-day period. We commit in advance to a percentage of that amount to establish a bonus pool. The pool is then divided equally among all of the employees, including administrative personnel, shop/product personnel, and lot workers. You can establish different percentage levels based on responsibility or job function if you wish; however, make sure the split is equal within each category. In other words, giving salespeople a larger share than shop personnel isn't likely to create problems. However, giving salesperson Smith a larger share of the team bonus than salesperson Jones screams favoritism. The purposes of the plan will be defeated by favoritism.

When the target is achieved, make sure you get the most mileage from it. Call a company meeting. Cut separate checks outside of payroll for the gross amount of the bonus. Take the deductions on the regular payroll checks later—and be sure you explain in advance how this will be handled.

It is critical to write a separate check if you wish to get the most from this plan. Distribute the team bonus checks as soon as possible after the goal is achieved, between regular payroll dates. I cannot overemphasize the importance of a separate check. I have found that people are so much more motivated by the bonus when they can see it. If it goes on normal payroll, the motivational value will be diminished, if not completely lost, because the standard payroll deductions will suck it up. Many people start a new bank account and use their bonus money for the little extras in life.

When you hand out the checks, do it in front of everyone. Give the team lots of praise and acknowledgment. Make a big deal about it! In this manner you will get the most from your investment. We have tried to design the team bonus to be approximately 10–12 percent of each salesperson's total annual income.

Salespeople are very sensitive to compensation issues. Once you put forth a plan, be careful not to change it dramatically. You will also see that many salespeople began to see your incentives as "entitlements." To avoid this, make sure you are very clear when you set up any incentive that it is just that, not a permanent compensation plan change.

In considering these three elements of a compensation structure, you need to determine what is best for you based on your goals and objectives for your organization. Design a plan that is right for you and then standardize it. Never make special "deals" with different sales representatives. One thing we have learned is to never go backward on percentages with a salesperson. When you calculate the numbers up front, make sure you build in a little for upward growth and do not put yourself in a position where you have to go back to your salesperson and reduce the percentage. Nothing is more de-motivating to a salesperson than having commissions cut. If you do find yourself in that position, the best method is to leave the plan intact and phase in the necessary changes with new representatives coming on board.

These are just a few ideas on designing your compensation plan for your salespeople. We recommend talking with your accountant, your lawyer, competitors, and similar industry businesses to find out what works for them. A good plan will attract and retain quality salespeople and make your job as a manager much easier.

BENEFITS

As a small company, we have always tried to offer big-company benefits. Many people are motivated by benefit packages and profit sharing. However, this is changing. Today's worker is becoming less and less concerned about those types of things and more and more concerned about income. Recently we have installed a cafeteria plan in our company. We establish a monthly dollar amount based on years of service; employees can use this amount to purchase health, dental, and disability insurance. If they already have coverage elsewhere, or choose not to have coverage, they can take a discounted cash amount. We have found this to be a great benefit to our employees. It has saved us money over simply providing major medical insurance and creates a tremendous amount of flexibility.

A number of companies offer these programs. I heartily recommend that you look into them. Two other benefits we provide for our employees are a 401(k) pension plan and a Section 125 plan.

The 401(k) has replaced our profit-sharing plan. We have great participation and offer a matching contribution for our employees who save in this manner. We also increase the match in a profitable year as a sort of profit-sharing plan.

The federally authorized Section 125 plan allows employees to deduct certain expenses such as childcare and noncovered medical expenses from their gross pay before income taxes are calculated. They save the income tax on those expense items and reduce their taxable income. It is a great plan, especially for single parents, and costs very little to administer.

SOURCES FOR RECRUITING NEW SALESPEOPLE

Let's examine where you find new salespeople. Where do you already look and where should you be looking? Look for potential employees all the time, not just when someone gives notice. Keep a file of résumés on hand so you always have several candidates to whom you would be pleased to make offers of employment. This way, when the need arrives, you don't have to make hasty decisions, pick the best of the worst, or leave a vital sales position unfilled for a long period.

However, a truth I have noticed over the years is that the salespeople I want working for me are usually working for someone else. We have all heard the old saw, "Keep the pipeline full of qualified applicants." Often this is unrealistic and self-defeating. Effective salespeople who are unemployed will not stagnate in a pipeline for long; those who lack the skills, motivation, personality traits, and persistence to be effective salespeople will remain in the unemployed column the longest.

Personal Sphere of Influence

These are the regular areas you frequent in your personal life, such as volunteer groups, sports activities, church groups, personal fitness trainers, and the parents you meet in connection with your children's activities.

Merchant Recruiting When the going gets tough, the tough go shopping. One of my favorite places to target for recruitment is in the clothing sections of upscale department stores such as Nordstrom's. You will find young men and women who are pretty good with people, usually have a professional wardrobe, and often don't make a lot of money. If you approach them, do it in a way you won't get them in trouble with management.

"I've noticed you have a good way with people. It would be inappropriate to talk to you at work, but our company is in an expansion period and if you are not satisfied with your current employment or salary, maybe you would want to contact me. Here's my card. Feel free to check out our Web site or call me directly." I may do this once or twice a week during lunch, and I generate several return phone calls from people. We have brought a few people into the company this way.

Another way to prescreen people is to notice food servers in restaurants. At a restaurant I found a very successful representative, Brad, who stayed with us for a number of years. Tom Hopkins has personally offered employment opportunities to people who have served him and his wife, Debbie, dinner in restaurants. You get a preview of personality and certainly of customer service abilities without anything being added to your dinner tab.

Business Sphere of Influence

If you are active in your local chamber of commerce, other business-oriented organization, or in a service club, you will enjoy many opportunities to promote an informal salesperson exchange on a cost-free basis.

Salesperson Exchange Within your business network of noncompetitive firms, you probably know several managers. If so, you have an opportunity to develop a valuable exchange program. When you have current employees or people you are interviewing who may not be the right fit for your organization or product, but who still have great potential in sales, you could refer them to another company. In return, the managers you help out in this way will probably return the favor when they run across a person seeking employment who is not a good fit for them, or if they don't currently have an opening in their company.

Salesperson Duplication Create a referral program to reward salespeople or other employees of your company when they refer a new hire. Use a special performance incentive fund program (SPIF) to encourage referrals of new employees. To make this work well, you need rules regarding any compensation to be paid. For example, always require that the new hire be employed with the company for a certain period of time and meet a specific performance standard.

Don't learn the hard way and pay the SPIF to the existing employee upon hire of the referral. At our company, we give a small amount upon hire and then after six months, if the new hire is achieving the performance standards, there is another "cha-ching" to the employee who made the referral. This encourages the referring employee to mentor the new hire to hit the required marks, and thus foster teamwork. We have had much success in using gift cards for professional clothing. This enhances the salesperson's wardrobe while limiting the tax implications of the bonus.

Suppliers or Vendors Consider the salespeople who visit your office to provide services or products. The salespeople who are able to get you involved in their product demonstrably possess important sales skills and since they're calling on you, they are more likely than the average applicant to possess some understanding of your industry. Always be sensitive in approaching this source so as not to disrupt a vendor relationship.

Owners of Your Product The people you sell your products or services to are excellent sources of good salespeople. You may get to know their personalities, and even their backgrounds, just through the sales process.

Again, be careful not to disrupt relationships with your clients. In an industry such as real estate, you are selling a home to an individual in a single transaction, and that may be appropriate place to recruit. In industries where the client relationship is longer-term, you may run a big risk by recruiting a salesperson as you may lose the entire account. In our business, we have upset clients in the past when their employees attended our seminars, saw what our outside representatives do, and approached us for employment. Their managers get very insulted, thinking we are trying to steal their employees. We have made it a policy not to pursue new hires in this way, but it may be appropriate for you.

Media

Newspaper Classifieds Depending on your market and industry, this time-worn standby could be your best recruiting method. Everybody knows about newspaper want ads. They are always up to date, and many job hunters look there first. Costs are associated with using this resource, of course.

When you craft your newspaper classified, don't think so much about attracting the salesperson—rather think about how to attract the spouse of the sales professional. Focus on benefits, if you have them; and on reward and incentive trips, especially if the trips will be to exotic destinations. In this way—appealing to the spouses— you can attract salespeople who are unhappy with their current situations, but have not yet made a move.

Internet Searches I urge you to implement an Internet-based program for recruiting. We recruit about 80 percent of our salespeople through the Internet. This approach has the distinct advantage of attracting computer-literate salespeople—a must in today's high-tech society. You will find these Web sites well worth looking into:

http://www.careerbuilder.com

http://www.monster.com

http://www.jobing.com (primarily serves Southern California)

http://www.jobhunting.com

http://www.careerjournal.com

http://www.jobfinder.com

Web sites are notorious for appearing suddenly and just as suddenly disappearing without a trace. To discover today's best recruiting sites for your company, do your own Internet search.

One feature most sites allow is to run a keyword search of the host's database of applicants. By entering your competitor's name or industry words you can view applicants who have experience in your industry. I do want to caution you here. Not only can you conduct a keyword search on your competitors, but you can also list your own company name. I was recently looking through a popular site and imagine my surprise when I found one of my own salespeople listing his résumé online. I have learned that when salespeople decide they want to make a career change, they line up all of their options before they decide to give the company notice. In this case I was able to work out a plan to transition this team member and eliminate the surprise.

Internet Advertising While the Internet can be a great resource for new hires, be aware that you may attract people living outside your city or state. In some cases, this can be beneficial, but you need a plan for the hiring and reviewing processes for individuals who live far away. Relying solely on phone interviews is risky. You may want to require an in-person meeting; if so, decide your policy on who will pay the travel expense before you talk to applicants. You will also need to create plans for relocation expenses if you decide to hire someone who does not reside in your home market.

Recruiting and hiring needs to be a full-time, 24/7 proposition. You need to be proactive and not wait to begin when one of your sales team members gives notice. If you are not proactive, you will tend to absorb salespeople rather than recruit them. Following is a useful checklist that you can use to make sure you are covering the important elements of a effective, proactive recruiting plan.

RECRUITING CHECKLIST

- Run recruiting advertisements and use other sources to find candidates 24/7.
- Conduct a brief phone interview. Follow your first impression as a sales management professional.
- Administer an Internet-based behavioral assessment. Can they sell? Can they sell for you? Are they computer literate?
- Conduct at least two formal interviews.
- Treat them to an in-house experience/day-in-the-life. Let them see, touch, and feel everything about the opportunity.
- Check references and administer a *mandatory* drug test.
- Conduct a panel interview involving other team members *after* the references and testing show a quality candidate.
- Complete the hire forms: orientation, commitment, and agreement on first-year goals.
- Begin training and implement the training agreement.

SUMMARY

Recruit salespeople on a 24/7 basis. Doing nothing until you have to replace departing salespeople means you choose to have a painful dip in sales production. Avoid this by taking action on a regular schedule.

Building a strong sales force requires an all-encompassing system for maintaining a high level of motivation in your team. Never miss a chance to enhance your team's motivation.

Define what you want in a sales professional by creating Position Results Descriptions for your team.

Measure each member of your sales team against the Salesperson Behavioral Profile Checklist.

Make sure your sales force is being compensated effectively. Their earnings should reflect the value of their contributions as well as focus their efforts on meeting the company's sales objectives.

Increase your understanding of what salespeople want from the company and from its compensation plan.

Consider installing a three-tier compensation system that includes a team bonus.

Utilize all methods of recruiting salespeople, especially those that attract the computer-literate.

Immediate action plan: All members of your team can usefully be categorized as champions, stable producers, marginal, or challenged. If you manage a typical sales team of a dozen people, you will know offhand to which group each salesperson belongs.

Priority 1: Recruit replacements for the entire challenged group.

Priority 2: Schedule shape-up-or-ship-out interviews with each member of the marginal group.

In the next chapter we zero in on the techniques of effective interviewing and hiring, techniques that yield superior sales results.

3 RESULTS-TARGETED INTERVIEWING AND HIRING

Early in my career, I learned and for many years followed the dictum that it is not good etiquette to discuss money and benefits on the first interview. However, the Generation Xers now in the job market seem to want to talk about what's in it for them right up front. Generally, those types of questions made me feel like I was being interviewed; they also gave me the strong impression the candidates were more interested in themselves than in what they could do for the sales team they wanted to join.

The interview process has changed to a considerable degree since I was on the other side of the desk. When I first started interviewing for job placement, I felt like I was being interviewed for that job. Now it's as if the candidate interviews the company instead of the company interviewing the candidate, especially when the economy is strong. I no longer fight the issue of money and salary coming up early, but I do try to divert it in the first interview.

I tend to stick to a traditional interview style and process. When we consider a new salesperson for our firm, we use a three-step interview process.

THE COMMON DENOMINATORS OF A SUCCESSFUL SALES HIRING INTERVIEW

Managers who decide during the initial interview whether or not to hire the candidate will experience lower sales results and higher personnel turnover than would be the case if their hiring procedures were more deliberate. However, for several reasons it can be difficult to move more slowly.

You may need to boost sales quickly. This is probably the worst reason for making quick and risky hiring decisions because you can tie up your resources with people who are not going to be productive. Unless you ruthlessly weed them out, when you finally begin to bring in strong people, you'll have to put them in among a negative-minded group who shouldn't be there in the first place.

You are interviewing people who seem ideal. You're concerned about them taking another job while you are running through your entire procedure. If you have a well-thought-out hiring procedure of the kind suggested in this chapter, stick to it. The feeling that someone is right for the job should go both ways; if the applicant isn't as keen on joining your company as you are on hiring, perhaps the person isn't as ideal as you first thought. Develop a strong procedure and then have faith in it.

You are getting pressure to hire more people fast from higher authority. How you react to such pressure depends, of course, on how strong your position is with the company. Explain how you see the situation: You can't do your job well if forced into snap decisions in which the likelihood of disappointing results is high. Here is where you'll need to sell the efficacy of your hiring method. Urge taking the long view.

In every case, poor personnel decisions simply compound your problems. Your success as a sales manager hangs on the quality of the sales force you are responsible for developing.

Concentrate on doing this and the results will soon show. To achieve the strongest possible sales force, I recommend organizing a three-step hiring process.

FIRST INTERVIEW: FOCUS THE DISCUSSION ON THE CANDIDATES

The purpose of the first interview is to let me know whether each candidate is someone I will want to take a closer look at. We ask people about their strengths as employees, find out about their current job, review their work experiences, and chat about what they like to do in their spare time. We encourage them to do most of the talking. In this way I get a feel for their personality, their goals, and their mannerisms.

We came across an effective method of discovery in another seminar, one put on by the Sandler Sales Institute. We have incorporated this method into our first interview session. It's quite simple and highly effective: Ask candidates about recent purchases they have made.

If your product or service is a major purchase, such as a house, automobile, or wedding jewelry, ask your candidates about a recent major purchase of their own. Some will respond along these lines: "Oh, I went online and thoroughly researched the product. Then I went to several stores to look at what was available to make sure I'd get the best value for my money. I took my time so I would be sure of making a good decision." If your industry warrants a longer sales cycle and most of your customers require a longer process for the decision, this may be a match. However, if your industry is typically a one-opportunity close, then this candidate's performance in the field may be too tolerant of the "I need to think it over" response from potential buyers.

I am not suggesting hiring or developing high-pressure sales-people, only that you compare the personality of the candidate to your industry. In our industry, we usually have a one-opportunity close, so I look for candidates who are not analytical buyers and perhaps are more impulsive. When I ask candidates how they typically purchase, I'm looking for an answer along these lines: "Interesting question. Let's see . . . One day I was driving down the highway, not even thinking about a new car when I saw these balloons. So I drove in and they had free food! Three hours later I was in the dealership's finance office authorizing the paperwork. I don't really know what happened!" When salespeople with this kind of personality are faced with client objections or stalls, they are more likely to respond appropriately and close the sale!

Similarly, if your industry involves smaller purchases such as stereos or computers, ask your candidates about their latest purchase of a small appliance. Someone who simply breezed into a store and bought something off the shelves may be a better candidate for you than a careful, analytical sort of person.

The way people buy is typically the way they will sell most effectively. For example, when I buy a car it is on impulse. I used to drive a Jeep Cherokee, and thought a third row of seats would be handy for an upcoming event. I just dropped by the GMC dealership as I was driving by to check it out. About two hours later I drove away with a Yukon. I didn't go on the Internet, and I didn't visit other dealers; I just did it on impulse, and that's probably closer to my way of selling a product than the analytical approach some people naturally favor.

Also, if you have a unique sales process or target market, you need to get a feel for which candidates have the right personality to handle your sales situations. I recently read an excellent management book by Marcus Buckingham and Curt Coffman entitled

First, Break All the Rules. It has a short but profound premise: People don't change much.

On this first interview, you are narrowing the field to the candidates whose personalities mesh with your company's services and products. With the right fit, you will waste less time trying to instill the required qualities of mind in people who lack them and more time nurturing the mental and emotional predilections toward success in people who already possess them. If my first impression indicates the candidate may have what I'm looking for, I'll schedule a second interview with her or him.

SECOND INTERVIEW: SELL YOUR OPPORTUNITY

The second interview happens after you narrow down the pool of candidates and bring back the ones you initially think are a good fit. This is when you sell the idea of representing your company to them. Talk about salary and compensation, benefits, hours, and environment. Paint a picture of a day in the life of someone on your sales team. Make sure this is what the candidate is looking for or feels qualified to do.

Getting them to go out and generate new sales prospects will be a challenge. Oh sure, they will pay lip service in the interview about how much they like to prospect—but don't bet on it!

THIRD INTERVIEW: CONDUCT A PANEL REVIEW AND PROVIDE A DAY IN THE LIFE

I allow the candidate to spend time with other employees, getting other opinions on the team and the company, and see if they feel comfortable with the mix. I also provide a day in the life so a candidate will experience what the job will actually be like. I learned this the hard way a number of years ago with a young lady who hired on with Results. Because our compensation plan is primarily fee-for-service (commission), she was concerned about her income dipping until she could get up to speed and asked if she could do her training during the off hours so she could keep working at her existing job until she was ready to go full throttle with us. We really worked around her, had people come in early or stay late to get her training completed. On her first full day, she was in the office at 8:00 a.m. making phone calls. At about 8:15 she excused herself to use the restroom—and I never saw her again!

We quickly restructured the interview process to include an in-depth look at what the job will really be like. Candidates now sit for a couple of hours with an inside representative or go to an appointment with an outside representative to view our salespeople in action. At the end of the in-depth look, they will have a good idea whether they want the job, whether they are qualified to do it, and whether they like the other employees and the company environment. If not, they can tell me, "I don't think I'm cut out for this." It may make for a longer interview cycle, but when do you want to know they're not cut out to take on a position in your company? I want to know before I take the time and effort and money to train them and put them into the position. We recently interviewed a man named Al for an inside sales position. Everything checked out perfectly. His experience, his attitude, his references all were impeccable. We believed we had our next champion. As is our custom, we had Al sit through the "day in the life" process. To our dismay, Al came away from that experience knowing he did not want to do that type of work. While were extremely disappointed, we were relieved we learned this before instead of after we invested the time and money to get him trained and on the job, which he surely would have left within a short time.

GAINING A COMMITMENT UPON HIRING

Once you have completed your interview process and made the selection decision, you will want to make sure you begin this new relationship with the proper expectations.

If your sales team has more turnover than the Arizona Cardinals or your representatives have a hard time living up to your expectations, it may be time to take a good look at how clearly you convey those expectations. A Gallup Organization poll recently found that the number one cause of employees' failure is the boss's failure to convey clear expectations. Managers ask why their employees fail or leave, but they don't like the answer. I tell them that it's usually not the employee's fault. I tell them that it's the boss's fault. If an employee chooses to quit, he has really fired the boss. We have found that the best way to clearly communicate expectations is from the very beginning. Here are some quick ideas that you can implement to make sure you are both on the same page:

1. *Start early.* Begin communicating your expectations during the hiring process to ensure nothing is left to chance. During the interview, read the prospective sales rep a description of the standards and ask if there are any questions about what is expected of the person who fills the position. Watch the candidate's response carefully, it may reveal how well the new hire will abide by your standards.

2. *Do it yourself.* Don't rely on intermediaries to convey your messages to employees. When you do this, you not only dilute your message, but you can't be sure employees receive the message you intended. Communication between you and your reps should be

just that—between you and your reps, not between your reps and a third party.

3. *Get feedback.* Don't assume that just because you've told your team what you expect of them, you've clearly conveyed your message. Get some feedback. Ask employees to express to you their understanding of your expectations. Explain the results you're looking for, and then ask them to restate what you've said. Using the commitment form we will discuss later, put your expectations in writing and review them often with employees. When you fail to clearly define the results expected, you put your employees in a race with neither a track nor a finish line.

This section will share with you how to get your salespeople started on the right track as soon as you hire them.

The First Day

A new employee's first day makes all the difference. Think about the times you started a new job and the manager wasn't ready for you. You found yourself sitting in the lobby for a couple of hours; you might have been given a desk where nothing was set up for you yet. How did you feel? Disappointed? You were really excited, maybe a little nervous, and then you began to feel like they weren't even prepared to have you in their office.

The experience leaves you with a bad impression and some excruciating questions. *Clearly, this is a slipshod operation,* you think. *Management is obviously disorganized.* You wonder whether joining this firm was a serious mistake. *Are the other parts of their business this confused? If so, how long can they stay in business? Is giving my all to becoming successful here worth it if the company goes belly-up in a few months?* These are not concerns you want to inflict on a new salesperson.

We have an informal party when new people join us. We host a bagel breakfast or a team luncheon to make them feel very welcome. Recently, someone from New Orleans started with us. We brought in po-boy sandwiches to make the new salesperson feel comfortable, valued, and at home with us. A recent team member from Boise was treated to a baked-potato lunch. (Be careful here. The carbohydrate overload caused a serious work stoppage later in the day.)

However, be cautious in this situation. There's a natural tendency to set up the occasion so the new salesperson will be pleasantly surprised to find his or her food preferences were chosen. When someone from Kentucky started with us, bringing in Kentucky Fried Chicken seemed a sure bet—but our guest of honor turned out to be a vegetarian.

Many companies give goodbye parties for exiting employees, but we feel it's more important to give hello parties to individuals coming in. Retirement is a special case, but a goodbye party when someone leaves to pursue other employment serves no company purpose. If friends of the person leaving want to throw a goodbye party, they can always do it—on their own time.

Of greater importance than a welcome party is to have the new person's space available and some temporary business cards already printed. It's very easy to do with all the automation available. You can buy business card forms designed to be run through the laser printer and pulled apart. Be sure to have their e-mail and voice mail systems set up. This effort can make all the difference in helping new salespeople feel valuable and important to the operation of your company.

Once they feel important to the company, then you can get them committed. You can't ask them to make the commitment if you have not shown them your commitment to them.

Establish Specific Personal Goals

What does the salesperson want to achieve in his or her personal life as distinguished from career goals? What income level does he or she aspire to? Is a new car or home a goal? Is preparing financially for the arrival of a child, or for some other family activity, an important motivator? These personal goals will encourage your salesperson to meet the company goals. Because they are personal, the salesperson should never be pressured to share them with you as a manager. However, you should require the salesperson to at least commit the goals to paper.

Only a few months after I started working for Tom Hopkins, he called me in one day. He said he was impressed, thought I had a good future with his company, and wanted to talk about my goals.

I had never really thought about goals, so when Tom asked what I wanted to earn in sales and what types of things I wanted, I really did not have a clue. So he began with the basics. What kind of car did I drive? My car was an aged Oldsmobile.

Tom asked if having a new car would excite me. I responded enthusiastically. Asked what kind, I said anything new would be okay. He then taught me the value of being specific, and we settled on a gold Jaguar. We determined how long it would take me to save the money for the initial investment and be able to handle the monthly amount. We set benchmarks, determined activity goals. I was excited!

After we finished he asked me to go to lunch, which naturally led me to believe I would be lunching with the company's president. Guess where we ended up fifteen minutes later? You guessed it: the Jaguar dealership. Within three hours I had ordered the car! Guess what comes with the car? Right, the monthly investment. Then and there I learned how Tom Hopkins motivated his salespeople. He got them in debt. But in my case it worked. I worked harder than ever before and pushed myself to do things I had never done. I not only earned far more; my skills and confidence grew rapidly.

Establish First-Year-Income Goals

Here's the most critical issue: the establishment of matched expectations with a new salesperson. This is also the area where many sales managers get into trouble. Let's say you know that a realistic first-year income in your organization is, let's say, $60,000. Sure, you have a 100 percent commission opportunity, and perhaps there is no ceiling to what a salesperson can make. (There may also be no floor). You discussed the compensation plan with the candidate prior to this step, so you would have asked him what he would like to earn in his first year. He responds with $120,000. You have an obligation to "lower his sights without crushing his vision."

Can you see where you can get yourself into trouble here? If you do not make the effort to put reality firmly in place, you set yourself up for a serious challenge ninety days down the road—or sooner. At some point, if that particular salesperson is not on track for $10,000 per month, he will be asking himself whether he was sold some blue sky. The ones most likely to quit over this issue are those with the greatest potential.

When discussing first-year income, you need to say (if it's true), "I think a goal of $120,000 is very doable. However, most first-year associates need to develop their skills and book of business, and generally they earn around $60,000. If you are earning $60,000 and are on your way to $120,000, you are okay with that, aren't you?" In this way you establish the proper expectation. Conversely, if you ask a candidate what she is looking to earn and she responds with $24,000, then perhaps she is not hungry enough. Setting the proper expectations early in the area of income will go a long way toward avoiding problems later.

Establish That They Are Coachable

Set up clear guidelines; establish when you will want your sales-people to listen to direction and how you will give them direction. Many salespeople wish to be independent, and even perform better when allowed to manage their daily routine. Make it clear, however, that you will have some coaching time. If they feel they are not getting enough of your time, or need your help, be sure they know how to go about requesting and scheduling it. The commitment must go both ways.

Confirm That They Will Follow Company Procedure

Make sure your team members understand the important weekly or monthly deadlines for paperwork. Give them clear guidance on filling out paperwork, who gets specific paperwork when it's filled out, and where to go, other than to you, when they have challenges or questions with procedures, benefits, or salary issues. We have found that in our company, as well as many companies whose managers I have spoken with, that new hires are never more agreeable and willing to commit to the company line than they are in the first few days. This is why it is so critical to confirm that they will follow your system from day one.

Validate the Agreement in Writing Using the Commitment Form

Get your agreement with the new hire in writing. The key word in the previous sentence is *agreement*. Unless the salespeople are in full agreement with the goals, and believe the tools they have to work with are adequate to accomplish the desired objectives, this procedure has little chance of having a lasting impact on sales results.

Develop a commitment form (C-Form) get comfortable with it, and introduce it into your hiring procedure. Introduce the C-Form in your hiring procedure, and get comfortable with it. Then incorporate the C-Form into your review process. It's a great way to recommit your existing salespeople and to create continuity of effort from them. Anytime performance weakens, the C-Form is a powerful way to get your sales force back on track.

Use this exercise right up front to establish what you expect from your team members and what they can expect from you. Capture all the vital information and agreements up front in writing,

---

MANAGER'S COMMITMENT

Date _____

I hereby agree to do everything necessary to help_____
                                                  (candidate's name)
achieve the goals we have mutually agreed upon this day and have entered into his/her file.

Approval _____

SALESPERSON'S COMMITMENT

I hereby agree to let _____ do what is
                              (sales manager)
necessary to help me achieve these agreed-upon goals. I also realize my production is affected by certain activities that have been proven to work. These include punctuality and attendance at all company meetings and using the tools the company has created to ensure my success. I also recognize my responsibility to keep a positive attitude, to maintain my enthusiasm while in the presence of other salespeople, and to avoid jealousy, gossip, and negative thinking.

If I am not living up to these commitments, I expect management to help me to recommit to these agreements and my goals.

Approval _____

and get solid commitment from your salespeople. Then you can move forward, and from day one it's clear that in forty or sixty days there will be a review. If things are not progressing as desired with a particular salesperson, you have a document, signed by both of you, on which to base the discussion of how he or she will get on track.

Obviously in the game of recruiting salespeople you have to go through a lot of people to find the quality or compatible ones. Remember, you have to kiss a lot of frogs to find a prince.

Commitment Checklist

- Get a commitment that the salesperson has accepted the position.
- Set a goal for first-year income and break it down to the monthly activity you have found necessary to reach the productivity goal.
- Have the salesperson set personal goals for the benefits of high performance, such as vacations, cars, toys, and so on.
- Have the salesperson commit to following procedure, attending meetings, and maintaining a teachable spirit with a positive attitude.
- Determine how the salesperson would like to be led and what things you can do as the leader to create the best environment for the person's success.
- Complete a written commitment form.

Here is a good example on how this dialogue might actually play out.

Let's assume you have completed three interviews with an excellent candidate named Jon Foxgrove, and you are almost ready to offer him a position with your firm.

You: Jon, I'm pleased to hear you want to earn $120,000 in your first year with us.

Jon: Are you saying it's doable?

You: It's not uncommon to hit your figure in the first year. Several of our present team members have done it; a few have done better, and of course, some haven't. It all comes down to reaching your productivity goals. Most first-year associates earn $60,000 to $70,000 in their first year. If you earn that figure, but can see where you can earn your goal of $120,000, are you going to be satisfied?

Jon: Certainly, I figured it would take a little time to learn the business and ramp up. Also, I've seen your productivity expectations and I've talked privately to several members of your team. I feel pretty confident I can do what it takes in this sales position.

You: What are your most important short-term goals?

Jon: I only have one. My wife and I want to take our kids to Hawaii for a couple of weeks as soon as I get rolling and have things nailed down in this new position. If I'm hitting the productivity goals, you won't object to me taking so much time off so soon, will you?

You: If you're hitting the goals, your time is your own. I only get uptight about time off with people who aren't meeting expectations.

Jon: That's what I wanted to hear.

You: I have a management commitment form I want to go over with you. This allows us to put each of our expectations in writing so we are clear about our working relationship. We find it solves a lot of potential challenges. Let's go through the process together.

Take Jon through the process of committing to his success with your firm.

People deserve to know what is expected of them. If you fail to make your expectations clear, how can you blame anyone for not meeting them? Important things you may feel are too obvious to mention might easily be the missed by newcomers struggling to quickly learn everything they need to learn and how to do everything they need to do. Explain performance standards in addition to describing the results expected of anyone occupying his or her position.

A SALESPERSON'S FIRST FEW DAYS

Unless you make yourself available to answer questions during the first days of new hires, they will ask the other salespeople. But since the members of your sales team are busy pursuing their own goals, they tend not to welcome being interrupted by questions and requests for guidance that are management's responsibility.

Position Results Description

Yesterday's way to define a position was to list the duties it involves: call customers, solicit business, take out the trash, and so on. Today we define a position by the results expected. This might be: "to generate X amount of revenue." We discussed this in a previous chapter, yet now is the time to implement this with your new hire.

When you write your position results descriptions, be concise. Identify the principal results or result desired. The fewer the words, the greater their impact. Find another place to emphasize the importance of other attributes of a top-notch employee, such as promptness, courtesy, enthusiasm, and so on.

You Never Get a Second Chance to Make a Good First Impression on a New Hire

The office image and work commitment created in the first few minutes of the new hire's first day is difficult to change. Whatever this impression is, it will probably be reinforced during the rest of the first day, first week, and first month. By the end of the first month, the original impression has hardened into a mind-set that is almost impossible to change. Thus the path to success and a long stay, or to failure and a short stay, is usually taken early.

Never start new people until you have the personal time to commit to them. One of the worst things a manager can do is schedule a new salesperson to begin and then not have a training plan for them, or worse yet, be personally unavailable to lead the initial training. Make sure you plan carefully so that the new hire is not sitting in the lobby waiting for you to take them through the initial process. Make it a priority in your planning and unless the building has caught fire, be available to begin the training. Remember, one of the most important things you need to do with new salespeople is to make them feel important and glad to have made the decision to join your team.

Everyone in the first thirty days wonders if they have made a mistake in joining a new group. I have heard this from other management trainers and found it to be so very true in my own management experience. It's especially true when you recruit salespeople that are already gainfully employed at another company. If you woo them away to join your firm, you just need to accept that they will have second thoughts within the first month. This is a great reason why you should try so hard to make sure they feel important in the first few days with your group.

Help each new team member to establish success as soon as possible after joining you. I believe this is very important. I also believe that feeling success early on does not necessarily mean making a sale, although that is a great example of success. Perhaps it simply means that the salesperson completes an element of the training successfully, such as a written review or a mock sales presentation whereby you are able to give them positive feedback. Any element that the new hire completes where you can give them positive feedback is a great example of helping them to see success early.

Implement the training agreement. I believe it is very critical that you set up a training agreement that outlines the expectations of and provides a checklist for a new salesperson training program. In many organizations, no such agreement or checklist exists. Yet, as we have stated many times in this book so far, new salespeople deserve to know what is expected of them. For example, when a person joins your group and completes the in-house training on sales and product knowledge, what are the expectations once he or she arrives in the field to do sales presentations? In our group, we clearly establish these expectations up front. Once our field salespeople complete the initial training in the office, we take them into the field for training. We clearly set up that the first presentation will be one where they will watch the trainer. For the second presentation in the field, we let them know that they will start and go as long as they feel they can. At the point they feel uncomfortable, they are to turn the presentation over to the manager or trainer to close.

The third presentation has a bit of a twist. We tell them that they are responsible for the presentation on their own and the trainer will watch. To make things extra difficult, we also let them know that the trainer will not intervene in any way, no matter how much the new sales associate messes up. This step is particularly difficult for the trainer because it means they have to in essence burn a sale.

Unless we take this measure, the new sales associates never learn how to work themselves out of a tough spot. I have also found that unless the manager teaches the salespeople how to work from behind, they may never feel they can do it alone and will continue to ask the trainer to accompany them on sales calls. I remember when I was going through my private pilot training. According to government regulations, before prospective pilots can earn their license, they have to take a solo cross-country flight. This means that they have to take off, land at an airport over fifty miles away, travel to another airport and then return, all by themselves. Since they are on their own, there is nothing an instructor can do but hope they did a sufficient job of preparing and training the pilot. I imagine that would be a very gut-wrenching time for any instructor.

I have also gone one step further, though I can tell you this is not for the trainer who is faint of heart. After the third training session, take the new recruit out a fourth time and let them know it is their presentation. Then, about half way through, you as the trainer say something stupid that would put the sale in jeopardy! Then watch how your salesperson works out of that challenge.

The most important concept here is to clearly outline the training agenda, who is responsible for which check-off items, and what you expect the salesperson to be able to do at various intervals. Here is an example of how we use this in our group. Obviously the language is specific to our industry, though I believe you will get the idea. Feel free to modify this training agenda to your company's training regimen. Work on your own industry needs and company objectives, but be clear about what you expect. Make sure the new recruits know what is expected of them. To have a stable, high-producing staff, each new team member must immediately be aligned to the mission.

TRAINING AGENDA

To: Nick Newhire

Objectives:

1. By Thursday, December 11, we expect you will have the actual sales meeting presentation memorized and be in a position to work on refinements. If you do not have the presentation memorized and at a point of seamless flow, then we can not help you further, and may elect to not send you into the field.

2. By Friday, December 12, you should have a complete and thorough understanding of our system of sales presentations and completion and be able to work competently with the computer software, to send and receive e-mail, and to synchronize your database.

3. By Monday, December 15, you should be able to conduct the sales presentation on your own and be able to complete all activities as described in the Position Results Description.

Dress:
Thursday, December 4, and Friday, December 5: Business casual

Monday, December 8, and Tuesday, December 9 (taping): Suit and tie (The impression made for your team should be positive.)

Wednesday, December 10, through Saturday, December 13: Business casual

Tuesday, December 2
8:30 a.m.–6:00 p.m.   Attend Tom Hopkins sales seminar

Wednesday, December 3
Travel day to Arizona. We will reserve a rental car and a room at the Marriott Fairfield Inn on Scottsdale Road at Thunderbird (southwest corner).

Thursday, December 4

9:00 a.m.–12:00 p.m.	Orientation and training in our marketing system, and the role of a salesperson. Field training with Ron in salesperson orientation.
12:00 p.m.–1:30 p.m.	Lunch break
1:30 p.m.–4:30 p.m.	Tom Hopkins sales training/product knowledge (DVD series)

Friday, December 5

8:00 a.m.–9:00 a.m.	Observe phone presentations with inside team.
9:00 a.m.–10:00 p.m.	Field sales training, prospecting, and referral generation
10:00 a.m.–12:00 p.m.	Tom Hopkins sales training/product knowledge (DVD series)
12:00 p.m.–1:30 p.m.	Lunch break
1:30 p.m.–4:30 p.m.	Training and overview of the sales presentation

Weekend on your own

Monday, December 8

8:00 a.m.–9:00 a.m.	Observe phone presentations with inside team
9:00 a.m.–12:00 p.m.	Tom Hopkins sales training/product knowledge (DVD series)
12:00 p.m.–1:30 p.m.	Lunch break
1:30 p.m.–3:00 p.m.	Field sales presentation taping and closing work with Ron
3:00 p.m.–4:30 p.m.	Actual sales calls; computer and CRM software briefing

Tuesday, December 9

8:00 a.m.–9:00 a.m.	Observe phone presentations with inside team
9:00 a.m.–11:30 a.m.	Training on the actual sales presentation; taping
11:30 a.m.–1:00 p.m.	Lunch break
1:00 p.m.–4:00 p.m.	Sales presentation review/feedback of recorded session

Wednesday, December 10

8:00 a.m.–9:00 a.m.	Observe phone presentations with inside team
9:00 a.m.–10:45 a.m.	SalesLogix training with René
11:00 a.m.–12:00 p.m.	Field logistics with Maureen
12:00 p.m.–1:00 p.m.	Lunch break
1:00 p.m.–2:30 p.m.	Employee briefing with Irene *(Bring your driver's license, insurance verification, and social security card.)*
3:00 p.m.–5:00 p.m.	Briefing with Tom on field issues, compensation, reports (metrics), and Position Results Description

Thursday, December 11

8:00 a.m.–9:00 a.m.	Observe phone presentations with inside team
9:00 a.m.–10:00 a.m.	Final Hopkins product knowledge exam. Review with Tom. Plan on using the remainder of this day to rehearse the presentation, complete advance work (confirmation calls) on meeting scheduled in Fresno, and prepare for the following week.
7:00 p.m.–9:00 p.m.?	Open House at new office. Our entire team will travel to Arizona and this will be an opportunity to meet everyone on a social level.

Friday, December 12, and Saturday, December 13
Company-wide team meeting each day from 8:00 a.m. to 5:00 p.m. at the Results office.

Sunday, December 14
Travel day to Fresno to conduct sales presentations.

Monday, December 15, through Saturday, December 20
Conduct sales presentations in Fresno, California.

Initial Training Checklist

Beginning a new sales job means the new hire must learn many new things quickly, from where supplies are kept to people's names and, above all, how to meet the challenge of selling unfamiliar products or services to unfamiliar customers. It's easy for the newcomer to feel overwhelmed, and this can be the first step toward discouragement and failure. Confronted by all the newness, few new salespeople will be at their best. Use this checklist as a guideline to making sure you cover all of the important issues with your new sales team member. We have found that many things we take for granted, or perhaps don't even think of, are very important to the new hire. Health insurance is an example. Make sure you discuss your benefit package, if you have one, with them on their first day.

Imagine the new salesperson going home after day one. The spouse will ask how the day went. However, the following questions can be even more important to both of them. This means the answers are more important to you as a means of enhancing their motivation and commitment to your company. Of course, if your benefits disappoint them, the answers will have the opposite effect Here are the questions the spouse is very likely to ask:

"Honey, how long before we are eligible for health insurance coverage? Is it a good plan? Do we have to change doctors?"

While these issues may seem trivial to you, they are all-important to them. If you can provide good information, you will have a more supportive spouse at home for the difficult times.

The following is a training checklist that will help you help your new hire acclimate more quickly.

- Be empathetic. Say things like, "I know we throw a lot at you right off, but in a few days it'll all settle down, and you'll be a solid member of our team." List the

things new hires need to know in a handbook, titled
something like *Making a Fast Start with Us.* Give them
a copy before they come in for their first day on the
job. This is another little detail to demonstrate your
determination to do everything possible to help them
fit in and hit their stride quickly.

- Turn your orientation tour into a celebration. The little
extra time required to make new people feel welcome
and secure will be repaid many times over. As you tour
the office introducing new salespeople, give the new
hire a list of the associates, with the nicknames each
associate prefers.
- Arrange lunch with the president or owner, if possible.
- Explain the company's goals, office, and unit, and who
the key team players are.
- Explain work ground rules.
- Explain the employee benefit plans.
- Explain the new hire's position mission and current
objectives.
- Define the work assignment.
- Present education and training plans, by whom and
when. Negotiate the training contract.
- Present work standards, responsibilities and
authorities, reporting systems, and the productivity
expected.
- Make asking questions easy. Tell them where to go for
help.
- Help them be successful on the first day. Work closely
with them on their first calls and, if possible, pick some
easy ones for them to cut their teeth on.
- Debrief at first day's end. Schedule appointment time
for this important function.

- Organize the balance of the week. Help them be successful by showing how a successful week is organized.
- Show them how to organize the balance of their first month. Help them to success by demonstrating how a successful month is set up.
- Set quarterly objectives and quarterly progress reviews.
- Hand-deliver calling cards. Confirm e-mail/voice mail.

Early habits are difficult to change. Be as active as possible to make sure new people form positive habits from day one.

SUMMARY

The vital functions of interviewing, hiring, and starting new salespeople off strong should be carefully organized and carried out according to well-thought-out plans. Snap decisions to hire during the first and only interview results in frequent costly hiring mistakes. Most of those mistakes can be avoided by following a three-interview plan in which applicants are shown exactly what is expected of them and how they will work and in which hiring managers gain more insight into the applicants' strengths and weaknesses.

Probe applicants' buying habits to better understand whether they are a good fit for your operation. Make sure applicants fully understand the position's responsibilities and goals and fully commit to achieving them. Establish their personal sales goals and first-year income goals.

Document their commitment to meeting production goals and to complying with company procedure. Develop and follow a Commitment Checklist with each applicant being seriously considered; do this as part of the written file you create for each new employee. This file is an invaluable tool for future reviews and, if the necessity arises, for justifying a termination.

Once the hiring decision is made, the sales manager's involvement with the new hire, rather than being over, is just beginning. New hires' first-day experiences—and especially whether they are made to feel welcome and secure—have a powerful and lasting effect on salespeople's attitudes toward their new company. Try to put yourself in the new hires' shoes and see the new job challenges they face.

Set up the necessities for the new person in advance—calling cards, voice mail, work space, and so on—so every new hire feels valued and can go right to work. Help them be successful on their first day by working closely with them.

Schedule time for a debriefing session at the end of each new hire's first day. Good habits learned early tend to stick with people; bad habits acquired early are hard to eradicate. Do everything you can to make those early habits good ones.

4 TRAINING YOUR SALES ORGANIZATION TO PRODUCE SUPERIOR RESULTS CONSISTENTLY

Great management starts when they realize training is an
investment and not an expense to be cut.

—W. Edwards Deming

Training is a component of strong motivation. It is not something
you remove from your budget when times are tough. Don't throw
it overboard when the ship is in the middle of the storm; hold onto
it for dear life!

There are many times when leading sales managers train salespeople. Without up-to-the-hour training, your sales staff will miss
many sales opportunities because they aren't prepared to cope
effectively with new issues, new concepts, or new product lines. In
many industries, this calls for almost continuous training in order
to enable the staff to exploit the positive new developments for
maximum advantage and minimize the damage inflicted by negative new changes in your competitive situation or the economy.

In this regard it's important to know yourself. The emotional
makeup of some managers causes them to respond strongly to positive developments and gloss over the negatives; other managers

do the reverse. Consider whether you have a balanced reaction to change, and give adequate attention to both negative and positive developments in spite of your natural tendency to favor one or the other. Doing this effectively calls for deep introspection.

WHEN SHOULD YOU TRAIN?

When You Recruit New Salespeople

This is a given: You have to bring new people up to a certain basic standard of skill or competency before putting them in front of your clients. Unfortunately, this is generally the only time when most companies conduct training for their salespeople. The best companies we have seen not only conduct initial basic training, they never *stop* training. This happens only when management is strongly committed to making it happen and is also determined to make the necessary resources available.

Before Strategic New Product Launches

Ongoing product-knowledge training is the key. Remember the last time you intended to make a sizeable purchase and asked the salesperson what the product could do. If the salesperson was pretty clueless, didn't you feel less inclined to buy? It's vital to keep your sales force informed on product updates and new models. Fast technology advances make it imperative to continually update the training of salespeople to keep them abreast of new products and trends.

How many times have you gone into a computer retailer or computer store only to discover you know more than the store's sales associate? Frustrating, isn't it? Regardless of your industry, product or service, always train your team on new product developments so they can effectively communicate with and persuade your customers.

Before a Large Advertising Campaign

If you are launching a new promotion or marketing trend, your salespeople have to be able to answer questions about specifics. While at Sundowner Trailers, I missed this opportunity in a big way. In an effort to increase the kind of customer who would purchase a living quarters trailer, we launched an ad campaign that mirrored the automobile industry. A living quarters trailer has an RV-style living area in the front of the trailer and the horse compartments in the back. They range from $30,000 to $100,000, depending on size and upgrades.

Buyers can pay the full price in cash or finance the purchase with monthly payments. To market to the finance buyers, Sundowner offered an introductory model at about $32,000 with a monthly payment plan. The campaign worked, generating many phone calls to the dealership. However, we failed to educate the dealers on the different approach needed for finance buyers. So calls went something like this:

"Hey, I'm interested in this new Aztec Trailer at $295 down and $295 a month," a finance buyer would say.

"Oh, yeah. We have three of them on the lot. They cost $32,500," the dealer would respond. Needless to say, we missed quite a few sales opportunities after investing about half a million in this sales campaign. The reason? Finance buyers don't want to know the total investment. It may even scare them. But they know how much they can afford monthly.

During a Crisis

When the company isn't doing well, you need salespeople whose competence skills are of a higher order. The quickest and most cost-effective way to achieve this is to intensify training of your existing staff. A few years ago Federal Express suffered through a labor dispute and subsequent strike. With the fierce competition in the package-delivery industry, FedEx was threatened with the potential loss of many valuable customers. However, Federal Express consistently trains their salespeople in consultative sales-training techniques, and this helped the company through its strike crisis. The commitment to ongoing training did much to avoid the potential disaster.

As the Market or Industry Changes

The pervasive presence of computers and technology in every area of business and in many aspects of personal life means your salespeople are under more pressure than ever to keep up with the times. The following are some ways to anticipate the next wave of change before it breaks over your team so that you can train them how to benefit from it.

1. Read your industry's trade journals.
2. Clue into industry-specific Internet newsletters.
3. Read futurist authors such as Alvin Toffler and Faith Popcorn.

Train All the Time!

Above all, Thomas Watson of IBM trained all the time.

—Peter Drucker

Our company is in the business of training. We provide companies with programs and seminars to help their salespeople improve their abilities and incomes. I am always amazed at what some sales managers might ask in an effort to object to investing the money it takes to attend training. The question I've heard most frequently is, "What if I train my salespeople, spend all that money, and then they leave my company?"

A question with far more impact on the bottom line is, "What if I *don't* train them, and they stay?"

CREATING AND MANAGING YOUR TRAINING PROGRAM

The key objective of any training program should be to develop team members to the point where they can do the job on their own. The worth of every aspect of the training program should be judged on the basis of how much it contributes to effective independent action.

Training and Leadership Styles for the Manager

With a new hire, most managers will generally use a directive style of leadership and training. In other words, they will tell the salesperson exactly what to do. They will direct the number of calls, schedule arrival times to the office, and give very specific directions on what to say to potential customers.

As the new salesperson gains confidence through training and in-field experience, the manager should move toward a coaching style of leadership. As direction becomes less specific, the salesperson becomes more self-directed.

As their skill level increases, most salespeople will perform better when their leader uses a supportive style of leadership and training. This is a critical element in any training program. In the current marketplace, many companies are minimizing the levels of middle management and flattening out their organizations. Most management books will tell you that the most effective span of control is between nine and twelve people. After that, the manager will lose efficacy. In today's marketplace, managers are routinely called upon to manage larger groups of frontline salespeople. The only way to make this work is to train managers to delegate the sales role. In the supporting style of leadership, managers must teach their salespeople how to resolve problems and challenges. Unfortunately, many managers have a difficult time letting go and they micromanage their salespeople. When salespeople bring challenges to the manager, the essential response in this phase is not simply to solve the problems, but to facilitate the solutions in such a way that the salespeople learn how to deal with similar issues on their own.

In management as well as life we teach people how to treat us. By continually solving the problem instead of teaching the salesperson how to solve it, we teach them to always bring the issue to management instead of taking care of it personally. Managers who keep themselves mired in this sinkhole will never be able to manage more than a dozen salespeople.

When training is successful, you can delegate tasks and objectives and the salesperson can accomplish the goal with little or no help from the leader.

We must also understand that the salespeople we train are at varying levels of capability. Every salesperson we hire joins our team with a different level of competency in sales. I think it is also important to note that just because some have been in sales for twenty years does not mean they have twenty years of sales experience. Some salespeople never learn from their mistakes and therefore they really only have one year of experience repeated twenty times.

Understanding the Competency Level of Your Team

Years ago a trainer by the name of Michael Vance, of the Walt Disney organization, refined some of Abraham Maslow's work and developed different levels of competency people go through in learning to become more competent. I have found these simple principles very useful in guiding the development of my own sales team.

Level One: Unconsciously Incompetent. This is one of the most difficult levels to train. When a salesperson is unconsciously incompetent, it means he isn't aware that he doesn't know what he is doing.

When people do not know they don't know, they are often unwilling to learn. Sometimes you may find yourself in a position whereby you need to challenge certain salespeople to get them to realize they do not know it all. In other words, prove to them they do not know everything. This can be difficult at times and may prove risky; however, it may be necessary.

One of our clients who owns a newspaper decided she wanted to find out just how much her advertising salespeople knew about the product they sell. She put together a forty-question test on information about the newspaper she felt the salespeople should already know. She was amazed at how poorly her team performed on the exam. Most people scored so poorly, it was a wonder they could properly sell the advertising space at all.

Here's the most interesting thing about this exam: The most senior salespeople did the worst in answering the questions. While it confirmed the publisher's need to retrain her team, it performed another important task as a ancillary benefit. When she reported the scores to the group, it was obvious to everyone that they were incompetent, so she was able to move them from the unconscious level to the conscious level in a hurry.

Level Two: Consciously Incompetent. People at this level realize they do not know it all, they know what they need to learn, and they are trying hard to acquire that knowledge and those skills. Once people grasp the concept that they do not know enough and will benefit from sharpening their skills, they are ready and willing to learn. This is a most important step for your salespeople to make.

Level Three: Consciously Competent. They understand how to do the job well, but it demands intense concentration to achieve the desired results. This step is the immediate result of effective training. Your salespeople know what they need to do to be successful in sales. Sure, they may need to review the checklists, study the sales brochures, and double-check all the figures, but they can get the job done.

Level Four: Unconsciously Competent. Once salespeople become unconsciously competent, they no longer need to think about selling at a conscious level. Like professional athletes who no longer need to think about the basics before they engage in their sport, these salespeople close the sales and bring in the revenue with seeming effortlessness because it's second nature to them. Of course, one of the challenges with the unconsciously competent is that when they go into a slump, which they all do at some point, they often do not know what they are doing that causes the slump. It is therefore difficult to get things back on track without taking time to go back to the basics.

Another challenge I see quite often with client companies is that they train their new salespeople in the field with their unconsciously competent salespeople. Think about it—most companies use their top performers to demonstrate what is expected in the field of sales. We used to have our new salespeople complete the in-office training, then after about a week, we would send them out into the field with our champion, who was unconsciously competent. But when new salespeople observe the top closer in action, and afterward ask for an explanation or analysis, they are often met with comments like: "I don't know, here is what I say . . . just say what I say and you can close the sale!" The top champion cannot articulate what it is she is unconsciously doing, and the new salespeople are left confused.

What we have found works far better is to have our consciously competent salespeople conduct the field sales training for new team members. They seem to be closer to the training and are able to more effectively articulate how to do the job.

Competency in one area of the job does not guarantee competency in all areas. A good example is the importance of salespeople understanding new automation and customer-relationship-management software applications. You may have a number of salespeople who can make a quality presentation and close a sale, yet cannot operate a computer. Salespeople who are good closers tend to spend so much time in the unconscious mode, arguing against the need for automation, that they never open their minds to become conscious of the need for a salesperson to be able to operate in a automated environment. They are unconsciously incompetent in that specific area.

Being quick on the draw in any situation is an important asset to a salesperson at any level of competency. In a supermarket, a woman asks a young produce clerk for half a head of lettuce.

"Well, I'm kind of new here; let me check with my manager about that." As the clerk walks up to his manager, he doesn't realize the woman has followed him.

"A stupid lady wants a half a head of lettuce." As soon as he speaks he notices out of the corner of his eye that the woman is standing next to him. Instantly he points to her and says, "And sir, this fine young lady here has solved our problem by taking the other half!"

After she leaves, the manager says, "Hey, you think quickly on your feet. We like that in our employees. We're opening a new store up in Canada, and we're looking for someone just like you to manage it."

"Canada. The only things coming out of Canada are tramps and hockey players," the clerk replies.

"Son, I'll have you know that my wife is from Canada!"

Quick as a wink the clerk says, "Which team did she play for?"

SIX STEPS TO AN EFFECTIVE, RESULTS-ORIENTED TRAINING PROGRAM

In working with sales organizations around the country we have found that is important to develop a proven model of training to provide to your salespeople. Be sure to customize the application of all aspects of the training to your specific industry and product. Here is a six-step approach to setting up your company's sales training program. In our company we use the Tom Hopkins "Building Sales Champions" system on DVD. It is a turnkey program complete with multimedia training, student workbooks, quizzes, a final exam, and a leader's guide. This proven program has helped thousands of companies improve their sales. The following steps follow the Hopkins program in sequence and will help you build an effective training program:

Step 1: Establish Expectations and Outcomes

Step 2: Create Emotional Involvement

Step 3: Get a Commitment to the Training

Step 4: Conduct the Training

Step 5: Test for Results in the Field

Step 6: Review the Initial Training Again

STEP 1: ESTABLISH EXPECTATIONS AND OUTCOMES

It is very important that your salespeople know what is expected of them during your training program. Equally important is for them to know what they can expect to gain from the training. At the outset of any training program, establish the gains you hope to realize from an improvement in sales competency, including company and team growth. However, do not forget to "sell" your salespeople on what the improvements can mean to them in personal income and lifestyle. By getting your team excited about the possibilities, you will have a more enthusiastic approach to the training and a much higher "buy-in" level from the participants.

It is also important to establish a benchmark of current sales performance so you can accurately measure the results your training is achieving. Many companies fail to take this very critical step. If you do not know where you are, then you will not know whether your investment of time and money was worthwhile and should be repeated or whether it should be changed. Take average sales numbers from your team over a period of six months to a year prior to the training, and then compare those numbers to the period following the training. In addition to productivity levels, it is also important to document activity levels prior to the training. Some companies will conduct training programs and not see an increase in sales volume due to external conditions, but they see marked improvements in closing ratios.

STEP 2: CREATE EMOTIONAL INVOLVEMENT

While the ultimate goal of any training program is to increase the level of competence of your salespeople, it should also be a time your salespeople can look forward to. We strongly recommend you develop themes for training. Make it fun! I recently conducted a training course for a large health insurance company in California. They had taken all one hundred of their salespeople out of the field for a day of sales training. They decided to make the theme of the day "'70s disco." They hired a disc jockey, created fun door prize incentives, and danced the Hustle on breaks. People dressed in '70s attire, and we had a blast. I was around in the 1970s, and it had to be the biggest fashion faux pas decade of the century, but there we were having a great time reliving those days of *Saturday Night Fever.*

You could also create a competitive environment. When salespeople compete for prizes and incentives as part of doing well in the training, they get much more from the overall experience, we have found. You could do something as simple as lottery tickets for participating in role-plays to a contest for the highest score on the final exam. I also highly recommend that you offer an incentive for improvements in sales performance following the training sessions. For example, you may want to offer a special bonus to everyone who exceeds their sales goal in the ninety days following the training. This is a great way to get your team excited about the actual application of the concepts, which is the most important part, isn't it?

Also, you should definitely create a plan for recognizing those who get serious about applying the material. One time we were training in the area of getting past gatekeepers and voice mail to talk to the actual decision maker. A few days after the first weekly session, Brad, one of our inside sales-team members, told me he had used one of the tactics, and it yielded him an appointment that resulted in a nice sale. So, how do you think I started the next week's module? That's right; I gave recognition to Brad and asked him to explain how the technique worked. I got a twofer on that one because I was able to build up Brad and sell the rest of the team on how effective the training can be when it is applied.

STEP 3: GET A COMMITMENT TO
THE TRAINING

Gain agreement that your team will take the program seriously and will apply the strategies and techniques shared as soon as it is practical after the course. This is something you will want to do in the very first session. Make sure they buy in and will work hard to learn the concepts that will be presented. It is also a great time to make sure people take the training seriously. One of the challenges many managers have is that when they introduce a new training series, they are met with reluctance by the crusty old veterans who do not believe they even need training.

It's important for your experienced salespeople to buy into the concept of training, especially if they also happen to be your top performers. How seriously they take the training can set the tone for the newer sales associates. One way we have found to get our experienced salespeople to buy in to the training is to delegate some of the training responsibility to them. In fact, according to many studies the person who benefits most from any training work is often the person conducting the training. Give part of the training curriculum (and adequate time to prepare) to your experienced veterans, and you will be amazed and pleased at how they will then embrace, support, and learn from your training initiative.

STEP 4: CONDUCT THE TRAINING

Once you have established the proper mind-set with your group, you are ready to begin the actual training sessions.

The following suggestions have aided thousands of other facilitators in training their people most effectively. The methods we offer here are not carved in stone; they are simple suggestions for how your people might benefit from the course. Your first consideration is what type of training program you are planning on implementing. It may be anything from an initial training course all the way to a refresher or recurrent training course.

Initial training. New salespeople who have had little or no previous training in professional selling skills will benefit most from this course. It provides an excellent source of knowledge about the basics of selling. It's also a great back-to-basics course for veteran salespeople.

Ongoing training. The program can help all salespeople review and bring back to active use effective but forgotten or neglected principles and techniques.

Individual training (self-paced). Individuals who are motivated to learn at their own pace can go as fast as they want without being held back by the instructor or by the rest of the group. Slow learners won't be intimidated by others who know the techniques. They can repeat a program as often as necessary before going on to the next session.

Group instruction. Many people learn better when stimulated and encouraged by other participants.

Once you have determined your format, then you must prepare to conduct the class. Your preparations should include the following:

- Review each segment yourself before teaching it to the group or individual. This way, you will be able to anticipate areas of concern for your salespeople or relate information on specific company policy. Perhaps you will also choose a particular product to be used during discussion or in role-plays after the session.
- If you are using a curriculum from another commercial trainer, such as Tom Hopkins, you will want to be sure to review the program. If it is a multimedia program, then view it in advance of the training session.
- Highlight areas in any workbooks or handouts to show where you would like to have your salespeople discuss their feelings or experiences. The case studies below include suggested questions to ask, areas to discuss, and role-play.

- If you are running an ongoing training session, review the highlights of the sessions already covered before you start the next module.

During the session:

- Provide some sort or workbook or journal to the participants. Be certain they fill in their workbooks.
- Have them highlight discussions or concepts that made them go "Aha!" in their workbooks. Then, they'll have everything in one place for future reference.
- Reiterate the highlights of each session from your notes and from discussion points.

At the end of each session:

- Ask your salespeople to relate any personal experiences they have had in the areas just covered.
- Ask your salespeople to refer to their notes several times between each session. Have them practice the techniques you teach on each other, on family members, and on friends so they become comfortable with them.
- Encourage them to use the material with their clients and report back the results to you. Your interest in their success will make them more interested in learning. It will also let you know whether they really understand what they're learning.
- Compliment them on their successes. Positive reinforcement will keep their interest in the program at a high level.

Create a positive learning environment. The environment we establish to help our salespeople learn is also very critical to effective training. You can have the best material and even be an incredible teacher, but if you do not set up the participants in a proper learning environment, or make them feel comfortable in the experience, you may get less than the expected results from your training program.

Although most of your students should have no difficulty learning from you, they will be influenced by the environment in which you are trying to get them to learn. This environment consists of the physical setting as well as the emotional atmosphere. If the environment is incompatible with the person or the job at hand, the chances of success are diminished.

Your attitude and behavior as the instructor is crucial. Your students must be treated as equals, without any hint of criticism for their attempts to learn. Here are some special areas to avoid and ones you'll want to develop to improve the learning environment.

Priority of Meetings

The success of the group meetings will depend a great deal on the importance the participants attach to them—and that, in turn, will depend a great deal on the importance you attach to them.

Give these meetings top priority, and arrange schedules accordingly. If you think these meetings are the most important thing that's happening, the participants will think so too. Schedule the meetings well in advance, and communicate the date and time via written memos or e-mail. One way you can demonstrate the importance you attach to these meetings is to have the room and materials fully prepared before the participants assemble.

Attendance

It is always tempting to excuse absences or to excuse people during meetings to handle important business, and sometimes this can't be avoided. However, it will pay to announce policies for attendance in the very beginning and make as few exceptions as possible.

Size of Group

The best results seem to be obtained when trainee groups are composed of ten to twenty-five people. There are distinct advantages to including some beginners and some veterans in each group. Beginners will get the benefit of experience, and veterans will be pleasantly surprised to find how much their own thinking is clarified by helping the less experienced.

Duration of Meetings

The actual duration of the meeting will depend on the quantity, importance, and relevance of what you have scheduled. Experience shows that enthusiasm mounts as the participants recognize the personal benefits of the discussion, and they may actively desire more time. Meetings that increase productivity are time well spent. Remember to schedule adequate breaks for participants. You should never exceed ninety minutes of class time without a break.

Classroom Management

The physical setting must be comfortable with respect to furniture and equipment, and free from external distractions that will interfere with learning. It is extremely helpful if the room is set up in such a way that everyone is seated at a table. This makes it easier and more comfortable for students to write in their workbooks.

You may want to arrange the tables in a horseshoe or semicircle so the participants can all see each other, which greatly encourages and facilitates participation. However, if control is critical, you may want to have the chairs and tables facing forward for a more formal atmosphere. Make sure everyone can see and hear the video and instructor without having to strain or constantly rearrange seating.

Physical discomforts and distractions can usually be prevented with a minimum of planning:

- Is the room too large or too small for the group?
- Is the work space relatively comfortable?
- Is the lighting adequate?
- Is the room too hot, too cool, or stuffy?
- Is there excessive noise to contend with?
- Are there other distractions?

Emotional Atmosphere

The emotional atmosphere must be supportive of the salespeople's efforts to learn. Everyone should have positive reinforcement from you and the other students. You will find that the most learning takes place when there is the best emotional interaction. When your participants feel comfortable and supported, they won't be afraid to express challenges they have applying certain techniques or doubts about whether or not a procedure works.

Make sure the learning and practice sessions are as free from stress as it's possible to make them. Your students will continue to learn if the session is a comfortable, pleasant situation for them. If they feel they have to give alibis or excuses why they haven't learned part of the material, they become defensive and start protecting their egos rather than learning and remembering.

Stress Each Student's Independence

You are there to facilitate the learning process—to set up schedules and outlines, to provide insight, answers, and direction. Help your students become self-directed learners and to be motivated to study on their own as a supplement to your instruction.

Encourage Your People

Many learning challenges are caused by a negative self-concept, and the self-concept is changed only by positive experiences. Even when they are having a difficult time mastering the techniques, students need to be encouraged rather than criticized. Use these situations to give them direction for the specific skills and techniques they need in order to succeed.

Let Your People Know You Are Pleased with Good Attempts

Everyone needs to succeed at something. Find positive things you can commend the students for and praise them. If they give good illustrations during the discussion period or report an attempt at using some of the techniques, encourage them even if they do not succeed at it. At least they tried. Praise them for it.

It is unrealistic to expect perfection, or that every goal be reached. When a student has failed to reach his selling goals, remind him that at least he is taking steps in the right direction. Suggest he review selected sessions before the next selling presentation.

Be Wary of Giving Excessive Praise

If praise is unearned, your students will know it and feel that you are not genuine. You can always find something to praise, but make sure it is valid. They will need at least some praise to keep themselves up, but too much can make some people dependent upon it.

Beware of Criticism

For the individual with a weak self-image, even constructive criticism can be damaging, even devastating.

This is especially important to remember during your discussion periods. Remind students that everyone is invited to make suggestions and express their thoughts and ideas, but any disagreement is expressed toward the idea, not the person. It is important to separate the person and the ego from the opinions expressed. Remember also that making mistakes is a part of the learning process. Help students to learn this approach to failing and to apply it to all aspects of their lives. Excessive attention to their mistakes only damages their self-esteem and further intensifies their poor self-images.

Know Your Students

A professional salesperson must know many things about his or her clients in order to give the clients what they need, want, and deserve. Likewise, professional trainers must know as much as possible about their students if they hope to be effective.

Help Your Students Know Themselves

Training programs can bring out a student's true values, feelings, strengths, weaknesses, and preferences. This might be an uncomfortable situation for some people. Their reactions to the activities will tell you a lot about them. During the discussion time they may discover and reveal personal values and problems that they may never have realized before. These sessions can result in real growth in both their personal and professional lives.

Accept Your Students as They Are

Everybody has talents and faults, strengths and weaknesses. Rather than trying to make your students conform to your expectations, use this training program to help them become the kinds of people they want to be. Some will excel in one area and never catch on in other areas. Don't criticize them for it, but help them make progress in the right direction.

Keep It Positive

It is important that students feel accepted by others. The best learning takes place in an emotionally supportive setting. If you sense negative attitudes developing, or if the group seems to be against someone or is making fun of someone, stop it as soon as possible. The participants are there to help and support each other, not to cause another person to stumble.

Avoid Humiliation and Embarrassment

Humiliation and embarrassment are caused by lowering a person's pride or self-respect; by making him or her uncomfortably self-conscious; by shaming, debasing, or degrading him or her; or by causing him or her painful loss of dignity. Procedures that lead to these conditions include

- publicly comparing a student unfavorably with someone else;

- laughing or smirking at a student's efforts, or responding sarcastically to someone's comments or questions;
- spotlighting a student's weaknesses by bringing them to the attention of the class;
- insulting or belittling a student's attempts;
- repeated failure. Occasional failure might motivate students, but repeated failure will lead students to think less highly of themselves and cause them to avoid the situation that has come to signify a lessening of self-esteem.

Avoid Frustration

Frustration is a condition or consequence that occurs when goal-directed activities are blocked, or when purposeful or motivated activity is interfered with. To frustrate is to thwart, to foil, to circumvent, to interfere with, to check, to make an effort come to no avail, to nullify, to defeat. Practices that can generate frustration include

- making no provision for adequate feedback and discussion,
- calling a halt when a student is absorbed with attempting to complete a project, and
- presenting information in larger units or at a faster pace than the student can assimilate.

The more motivated the student is, the greater the frustration when his efforts are blocked. We recommend you create and carefully follow an appropriate training schedule. Too much at once can be compared to the students who came to drink from the fountain of knowledge and got sprayed with a fire hose. We want to quench their thirst, not drown them.

Don't Create Fear and Anxiety

Avoid creating fear and anxiety, which include distress or uneasiness of the mind; apprehension of danger, misfortune, or pain; tension, foreboding, worry, or disquiet; and anticipation of unpleasant consequences.

Teaching procedures leading to fear and anxiety are those that threaten various forms of unpleasantness. They include

- telling the student by work or deed that nothing he can do will lead to success, and
- insinuating that contact with the subject will lead to undesirable consequences.

For example: "You won't understand this, but . . ."; or "It ought to be perfectly obvious that . . ."

Undoubtedly, your first reaction is that you would never do or say such things. However, you might have said it in a kidding way and without your knowing it, the student was offended or hurt by it. Be extra sensitive about your students' feelings.

Beware of Boredom

Boredom is caused by situations in which the stimuli are weak, repetitive, or infrequent.

A typical response is falling asleep or inability to stay focused. Procedures leading to boredom include

- presenting information in a monotone voice;
- rocking rhythmically back and forth while speaking;
- using impersonal, passive language.

One of the most important things I can share with you as a trainer is to keep your students involved in the training. Try and make it as experiential and interactive as possible. There is nothing worse than a "talking head" who does not involve the participants in the learning process.

Case Studies

One of the best methods I have discovered for involving students in the learning process and getting them to take "ownership" of the training ideas is to utilize a process of role-play and discussion involving case studies. Case study work is similar to the way we used to work out math problems in elementary school. Remember what your teachers used to do? They would create story problems so that we could conceptualize the numerical challenge and be able to see the math problem in terms we could comprehend. Case study work is an excellent method to get your salespeople to see the challenge as being real, to come up with their own solution, and to allow you the opportunity to guide the solving of the sales challenge.

The key to good case study development is to re-create the challenges your salespeople face every day, in their language and in terms that make them feel like "Yeah, this could happen," or "I've had this hit me in the face before!" In this manner, your salespeople will take the training seriously and come up with workable solutions they will use in the field. When your participants look at the case study and respond with, "Oh, this is not what really happens," what's the result? They discount the entire exercise. Great care should be exercised in developing true-to-life examples. The numbers need to be accurate; product descriptions and scenarios should all be as real-world as possible.

So let's say your training session is on a specific methodology for handling sales objections for your product or service. Once you have completed sharing the strategy or tactical approach, you would break the group into smaller groups of three to five people (depending on overall size of the group and time allowed for the exercise).

The next step is to assign each group a different sales challenge or case study. Let them discuss the challenge and come up with a solution that they will then role-play in front of the entire group. During the role-play you as the facilitator will redirect and coach them, reviewing the principles that were taught and explaining how they apply to the scenario.

We have provided nine case studies you may wish to use to get your people thinking about different ways to handle selling situations. The training you have given will provide a solid foundation for them to draw from. Consider copying the individual studies and having your students work on them in small groups.

The following case studies are presented in a generic manner and should give you a model of how these story problems can be constructed. As we have stated before, our experience in training has taught us that the actual case studies you use in your training should be built around your product or service. To create the most effective use, all product model references, investment options, and challenge situations need to be as accurate as possible. If the situations are not accurate, the participants tend to be distracted and discount the validity of the exercise.

There may be more than one effective answer for each situation. In some cases, it may be best to focus on how to avoid getting into the difficult situation. Other cases assume nothing you could have done would have prevented the situation from arising. In the latter cases, focus on resolving the issue. Keep in mind that there does not have to be a specific right or wrong answer for all these situations. The solutions can be as diverse and creative as your team chooses to be.

Case study scenarios can be used before or after the training session. In our experience, case studies are most effective after the training session; this allows the participants to see exactly how a certain sales tactic or strategy will fit into their specific business challenges.

Break your team into groups and have them discuss the case study scenario, brainstorm possible solutions, and prepare a response to share with the rest of the class. The reporting process can be as simple as a narrative on how the group chose to respond, or as complex as a role-play skit that demonstrates the response.

CASE STUDY 1

You are a customer-sales representative with Software Solutions, a major computer software company. You have taken a call from Suzanne James with ABC Manufacturing. She seems to be very knowledgeable and technically competent. She gives you a list of specifications and asks for an exact quote. You want to ask some more questions to make sure you understand and are accurately quoting the best system to meet her needs. She seems irritated and her response to your questions is that she just needs the numbers, bottom line.

Assignment
    a. How would you get this caller to give you more information so you can present the best solution?
    b. Outline your strategy and be prepared to role-play your solution to this sales challenge.

Facilitator's Note
Building rapport right away is important, yet it is also important to understand the buying behavior that this client is displaying.

The process that Tom Hopkins teaches in his sales training programs for qualifying would be a good transition into the more technical questions you need to ask to best serve the client. It is important in these situations to make sure you communicate to the client the fact that you do not wish to misquote her and therefore it is imperative she provide information to you.

CASE STUDY 2

You are a customer sales representative for Cars R Us Auto Sales. You're enjoying the sun on a beautiful day at your dealership. You're thinking that it's a great day to be driving around in a convertible when suddenly potential clients drive onto the lot in one. You greet Mr. and Mrs. Jackson as they emerge from their vehicle. They're interested in a minivan because his two children are coming to live with them. They're certain a minivan is the way to go because everyone else with kids seems to have one.

Assignment

    a. Develop your questioning strategy to determine the needs of these clients.

    b. Develop a triplicate-of-choice scenario to present to these clients after you have determined the best solution for their needs.

    c. Be prepared to role-play your response and presentation of the three options.

Facilitator's Note

It is important to understand the buying behavior that these clients are displaying. The process for qualifying would be a good transition into the additional questions you need to ask to best serve them. It will let you know their current automobile situation. It is also important in these situations to make sure you don't assume a minivan is best for them; perhaps an SUV would be appropriate in this case. It is critical you communicate to your team the value of determining the clients' needs and wants before you ever begin your presentation.

CASE STUDY 3

You are a sales representative for Yachts of Fun Yacht Sales. You receive an inquiry call on the new *Mainship 35* from one of the company's advertisements in *Northwest Yachting Magazine*. The caller does not currently own a boat and says he is a somewhat inexperienced sailor.

He informs you he is looking for a low-maintenance vessel and, while unsure of his budget, figures he will have to spend around $200,000 to get the kind of boat he wants. A doctor, he is married and has three teenage children. He and his family want to spend most of the summer cruising in the Puget Sound area.

Assignment

 a. Your objectives are to respond to this inquiry, qualify the client as to needs, and set an appointment to show him a specific model(s) that would fit his needs.

 b. Demonstrate how you would respond to this inquiry and schedule the appointment.

 c. Explain why the yacht you recommend would be a good choice for the client.

Facilitator's Note

Follow the process as a transition into additional questions that need to be asked to determine the best solution. Have your sales team write out the qualifying questions they would use. Work with them to make that process even more efficient by eliminating questions that may not be as important and restructuring questions so they get even more information from the client. Many salespeople will ask the same general question in different ways, which can be frustrating to the client.

CASE STUDY 4

You are a salesperson for Keep on Truckin' Truck Sales. You're showing a brand new Freightliner Century Class Truck to a prospective buyer. It is a stock unit and as equipped, the list price is $104,088. He is a new owner/operator just starting out, so he does not have a trade. The buyer says he will take it today if you will accept $95,000 for the truck.

Assignment

 a. Will you accept the offer?

 b. If not, what will be your strategy to sell him on the difference?

 c. Be prepared to role-play your response to this offer.

Facilitator's Note

This study is a great example of what many salespeople get caught up in and illustrates the importance of not getting drawn into a price negotiation until you are finished selling.

Help the participants to understand the difference between selling and negotiating and how to use an objection-handling methodology to respond. Make sure they isolate that the client wants the product and money is the only thing standing in his way. Then, you can select one of several closing phraseologies for handling money.

CASE STUDY 5

You are a sales account manager for Make 'em Pay! Medical Collections. You have been requested to submit a proposal for your company to handle all workers' compensation accounts for a group of hospitals in your region. You have built an excellent relationship with the business office director at one of the hospitals. After all the proposals are in, she discreetly lets you know that your bid on collection fees is nearly 2 percent higher than the next lowest bidder. Everyone was impressed with your company; however, if you could not "sharpen your pencil on the rates," you were not likely to make the cut.

Assignment

   a. Would you discount your rates? If not, what would be your strategy to justify the difference in rates?
   b. In either case, what kind of a presentation would you make in response at this juncture?
   c. Be prepared to role-play the specific response.

Facilitator's Note

Help the participants understand the difference between selling and negotiating and how to use an objection-handling methodology to respond. Make sure they separate these two issues and proceed on the basis that the client wants the product, and money is the only thing standing in her way.

CASE STUDY 6

You are a salesperson for Horsin' Around Trailer Sales. An experienced buyer comes into your dealership looking for a horse trailer. Based on your qualification questions, you recommend the Valuelite trailer. After showing him the trailer and discussing the finances, the buyer tells you he can get a similar trailer for $800 less at another dealer on the other side of town. He tells you thanks and makes for the door.

Assignment
     a. How will you get him to turn around and talk with you further?
     b. What strategy will you use to sell him on the difference?
     c. Be prepared to role-play your response to this challenge.

Facilitator's Note
Help the participants understand the difference between selling and negotiating and how to use objection-handling methodologies to respond. Make sure they isolate that the client wants the product and money is the only thing standing in his way. Then, you can select one of several closing phraseologies for handling money.

CASE STUDY 7

You are a representative of Always Ready Temporary Services. There is an accounting firm in your area that uses a couple of your competitors to staff the fluctuations in their seasonal business. You are new to the territory and have never been able to get in to see the office manager. The office manager's gatekeeper tells you she is happy with the vendor they are currently using. This has thwarted your call attempts thus far. Apparently, there was one too many "no call, no shows" in the past, and the office manager has blackballed your company. You realize it is a good piece of business and you want to reestablish the account. Besides, you learned so many good ideas at the recent sales training session, you just had to try one of them out.

Assignment

    a. What would be your strategy in handling this situation? How would you get the office manager to give your firm another try?

    b. Let's assume you finally get a five-minute stand-up meeting to introduce yourself. What strategy will you use?

    c. Be prepared to role-play the first few minutes and opening remarks of this presentation.

Facilitator's Note

This is a classic example of the client wanting to shut out the salesperson because she had a bad experience in the past. Use Tom Hopkins's proven "Put the shoe on their foot" strategy to reverse the situation. Remember the goal is to get a presentation with an open-minded client. No sense trying to sell the client at this juncture; just get back in for the fact-finding and presentation phase of the selling cycle.

CASE STUDY 8

You are an agent for Lifetime Financial Services. You have been following up on a certain client for a long time. He has been difficult to close and has been very concerned about money the entire time. You are finally able to close the sale, complete his life insurance application, and get a check for the first month's premium. You schedule the medical exam and feel proud of the job you did in handling this tough client.

    Everything seems to be going well until you hear back from the underwriter that due to a small medical challenge, you are not able to issue the policy as a preferred, but rather it will be issued as a standard policy. This increases the premium significantly; you will now have to go back to the client, explain the situation, and get him to agree to the higher premium. You know he is going to be upset, and fear he may cancel the policy.

Assignment

    a. What will be your strategy in speaking with the client?

b. How will you persuade him to keep the policy at the death benefit he previously agreed to?

c. Is there anything you could have done to prepare for this situation in advance?

d. Be prepared to role-play your presentation to this client.

Facilitator's Note
Run this scenario as it was presented, as it will be a great practice session for the real thing. However, this is an excellent example of circumstances where the best response is to not get into the situation in the first place. Use this type of exercise to build confidence in your sales team to not drop to the lowest rate too soon. In this example, it would have been better to initially sell the client on the higher premium and then if the lower preferred rate becomes available, you can surprise your client with the good news.

CASE STUDY 9

You are a loan officer with Simoleon's Mortgage Services and are contacting local real estate agents to build your business. At a local real estate board meeting you meet an agent whom you know is doing a large volume of sales. You would certainly like to have some of her business so you can show her what you can do. When you approach her to introduce yourself and offer your card, she simply says, "No thanks, I send all of my business to XYZ Mortgage, and I'm quite happy with the service I receive."

Assignment
a. What will be your response to this stall?

b. Be prepared to role-play your response to this objection and demonstrate how you would attempt to set an appointment with this real estate agent.

Facilitator's Note
This is a common stall in many industries. The best technique to use at this point is Tom's "History Readback Technique." Remember the goal is to get a presentation, not to sell them at this point.

GOOD SALES SCRIPTING

One of the most important things that can come out of case study work is the development of good sales scripting. Make sure you take advantage of the brainstorming activity you generate by capturing what is being developed for future use with new sales associates or future training programs.

In sales situations, words pour out of salespeople, most of whom are naturally loquacious. But do these outpourings of verbiage make the best presentation of the benefits your products or services offer? Close study of what salespeople of low effectiveness actually say in sales situations reveals weaknesses in some or all of the following areas:

- Sales effort begins before the prospect's needs and concerns have been fully developed due to poor listening. This often causes the salesperson to place major emphasis on issues of minor importance to the prospect instead of demonstrating how the product or service will meet the prospect's major needs.
- Issues are raised but not fully explained.
- Salesperson frequently jumps from one point to another without completing any of the thoughts, thus creating confusion in the prospect's mind rather than conviction to buy.

These difficulties can be overcome by developing scripts to cover the most common sales situations that will be encountered. The most effective way to put any sales point across should become a written script, the essence of which every salesperson should absorb. The goal is not to memorize these scripts word for word. Sales scripts learned by rote tend to have the off-putting sound of a canned speech when spoken to a customer. To avoid this, train your salespeople to include the salient points plus any especially convincing or pithy phrases. The goal is to make a strong presentation in their own words, one personalized to the individual prospect.

Scripts for handling objections are as important as those for presenting benefits and for closing.

STEP 5: TEST FOR RESULTS IN THE FIELD

Naturally, as you implement your training programs, you will want to check on progress and encourage application. To make sure your students comprehend the training ideas you have presented, you should have them complete a final exam on the material presented. I think it is an especially good idea to let them know up front if you intend (and you should) to test them in the end.

Another good way to make sure your training is having an impact on sales is to conduct follow-up surveys with clients to determine what level of improvement in sales technique has resulted from the training and to discover any parts of it not adequately assimilated by the trainees, or not well enough presented by the trainer. You should certainly go on an "inspect what you expect" tour with your salespeople. Go along on sales appointments; if you catch your salesperson using a technique, give him recognition for it. If you notice that a salesperson failed to use one of the concepts and it could have cost her the sale, let her know that as well (privately, of course).

Measure sales results against the established benchmark. This is so important. If you took our advice in the earlier chapter, you know where your sales were before you launched the training program. Now is the time to see how the post-training performance stacks up. If you find that sales have improved and you feel it is a direct result of your training efforts, make a *big deal* about it with your team. Make sure everyone knows that training works. Gather testimonies from successful applications to encourage other sales team members to continue in the training and to apply the presented concepts and strategies.

Before the beginning of training, you will have announced incentives for applying the training. Now, with evidence in hand to prove the effectiveness of your training, distribute recognition and the incentive awards. Make a concerted effort to recognize those who took the training you provided and enhanced their competence and thus their incomes.

STEP 6: REVIEW THE INITIAL TRAINING AGAIN

This is a great idea! It seems as though when you hire a new salesperson they are so overwhelmed with all of the things they are learning that important concepts fall through the cracks. After new associates have been on the team approximately six months, have them go through an abbreviated version of the basic training course again. You will be amazed at how they now realize the importance of the training they went through. It will make so much more sense to them after they have been in the field for a period of time. I know of many managers who conduct a brief initial training session with new hires, then they send them out into the field to get beat up, bloodied, and tossed around by customers. Then, and only then, they bring them back in to the office for a review of the initial training sequence. These managers have found that people truly understand the role at that point.

SUMMARY

Training is not merely a subsidiary program sales managers run from time to time when they're in the mood. On the contrary, training is the essence of sales leadership. However, unless done well, training is likely to be worse than ineffective. If your team feels the training was poorly prepared, didn't help them meet their challenges, or was presented under distracting or uncomfortable conditions, the training sessions are likely to be seen as a waste of time, thus lowering morale and respect for management.

Train when times are so good you're tempted to skip it because you're too busy; train when times are so bad you're tempted to skip it because you think you can't afford it. Train when you recruit new salespeople. Train when you launch a new product. Train before a large ad campaign. Train during a crisis. Train when the market or industry undergoes an important change.

Train all the time! But never carelessly, or too hurriedly to do it well. Careful planning, rehearsal, and preparation are essential to effective training. Impress your team with the brevity and bite of your training—with its conciseness and immediately useful content.

Look on training as a major activity you will do with constantly increasing effectiveness throughout your career. Organize your training materials from the start with a view toward never-ending improvement and augmentation. Plan to delegate parts of the training to your most successful salespeople, and provide sufficient recognition and other rewards to maintain their enthusiastic participation.

Begin by understanding the competency level of your sales team. Take a step-by-step approach to developing an effective, results-oriented training program. Create a distraction-free learning environment in which to conduct the training, and do so in an accepting, empathetic, and wholly helpful manner.

Use case studies to imbue the training with real-world vitality.

Prepare sales scripts.

Study the best ways and times to repeat basic training for new salespeople.

5 HOW TO RUN SALES MEETINGS THAT MATTER

THE ESSENTIAL INGREDIENT IN EVERY SALES MEETING

Sales managers who have decided to run a sales meeting because they have something important to convey have passed the first test for a successful meeting. They have a purpose! I realize this test seems obvious, but think back to all of the meetings you have been to that had no value or agenda whatsoever. I know I have attended many meetings where I just rolled my eyes and shook my head, thinking, "What a waste!" The first step to leading a successful sales meeting is to have a clear reason for calling one. Common reasons for holding a sales meeting are:

To inform the sales team—Give information on what is happening at the company, like a new product being announced or a new advertising campaign being launched, or discuss what is happening in the field.

To plan with the sales team—Discuss future goals and objectives, assess trends in the marketplace, and discuss how the company can plan to meet challenges.

To educate the sales team—Training is a critical component of any successful sales organization. I find the best companies make training and education a part of every sales meeting. Whether it is on the products your company offers or the skills your sales team needs to close more business, training is always a great reason to hold a sales meeting.

To inspire the sales team—Like training, inspiration and motivation should be part of every sales meeting, but sometimes the whole purpose of the meeting is to get people revved up!

To reward the sales team—Sales meetings are great places to bring everyone together to give out praise and recognition. Remember, however, to praise in public and criticize in private, as discussed in the beginning of the book. Never, ever use a sales meeting to criticize an individual salesperson. I have seen it happen and it is not a pretty sight. Use sales meetings only to praise an individual or team.

To build teamwork throughout the sales team and the company—Sales meetings can be excellent venues to build teamwork and to integrate parts of the company that don't always work together. When we plan our sales meetings at my company, we often work segments of the agenda into areas that the administrative team can participate in as well. We find this is a great way to build an understanding of what each group does so that each can have more appreciation for the other. I would highly recommend that you work participation time into your sales meetings if you have an accounting group, an installation team, a customer service team, or any other groups that work apart from sales. The payoff is a more understanding and cooperative organization.

WHAT'S THE PROBLEM WITH MEETINGS?

Effective meetings don't just happen; they are usually the result of a great plan. As we discussed in the chapter on motivating salespeople, too many organizations hold poorly planned and poorly run sales meetings, and it runs down the motivation of their teams. Instead of contributing to a sales organization's efficiency and production, they actually make the team less efficient and less productive. How many times have you heard someone complain about being stuck in some useless meeting or on a worthless conference call? With today's competitive sales environment, it is more important than ever before to make your sales meeting count.

Repetitive meetings are a waste of time. My discussions with sales managers around the country have shown that as much as 53 percent of the time spent in meetings, which includes time you spend in meetings, is unproductive. When you add the fact that most sales managers spend nearly a third of their workday in meetings, is it any wonder we don't get things done?

Here are five common reasons meetings go wrong:

- There are too many meetings. When did you last say to yourself, "I haven't been to any meetings lately, and I sure miss them"? You are more likely to say, "I can't get any work done with all these meetings!"
- Most managers don't do a good job of planning meetings ahead of time. They fail to prepare agendas or to communicate with participants about the purpose of the meeting.
- Participants are not properly briefed and come unprepared. If agendas are not distributed in advance and the participants are not aware of what is to be discussed, then how will they know what to bring or

how to prepare for the meeting? The ultimate result is time wasted while everyone stumbles blindly along trying to figure out why the meeting was called in the first place.

- The meeting is dominated by one or two know-it-alls. Every meeting has them, and they always take too much time trying to impress everyone by asking obvious-answer questions and generating side discussions. An effective sales manager knows to train people how to act in the meeting and does not allow this type of hotdogging. It usually starts when participants try to conduct "off-line" business during the meeting. You have seen it happen; old Bob jumps into the middle of the meeting and yells across the room, "Hey Joe! Did you close that lead I sent your way?" The great leader will stop that type of activity right in its tracks and get the meeting back on topic while letting everyone know that that type of behavior is not appropriate and needs to be handled another time.

- The meeting lasts way too long. Although we all know that a meeting should not last longer than it needs to, most managers let the meeting extend to fill the time allotted. So rather than adjourning to let the participants move on with the day when the important issues have been addressed, the meeting drags on and on and on.

The Cost of Holding a Sales Meeting

Sales meetings can be expensive as well as time-consuming. Meals, travel, and meeting space all require an investment. The real investment, however, is not so much the physical cost of the meeting, but the cost of the sales that are not being made because your team is not on the phone, in the field, or at a customer's office. Before you commit to a sales meeting, make sure you are aware of the investment you are making. You should also commit to a return value you expect from the time you have invested. Make sure the meeting provides sufficient value for the salespeople to quickly earn back the investment.

Where to Hold a Sales Meeting

Where you decide to actually conduct the sales meeting will be determined by the outcome you expect and the type of meeting you plan to conduct. If the meeting is designed to generate discussion and two-way dialogue, you may wish to hold it in your office with an interactive seating format. If the meeting is more about recognition or inspiration, then an off-site venue might be more appropriate, with classroom-style seating to keep the focus on the front stage area.

In-Office, On-site Meetings Holding the meeting at the office is clearly the most affordable method. It can, however, reduce the meeting's effectiveness because you will likely find it difficult to round everyone up at the beginning if they are at their desks, chatting with other staff members, or taking client phone calls. Another disadvantage is that during breaks, salespeople will likely go to their desks and check e-mail and voicemail, or perhaps even try to squeeze in a phone call or two. One of the things I have learned from planning and running sales meetings is that in many cases, some of the most productive time is not in the meeting, but during the social events or breaks of the meeting when the team can truly interact. I always plan for this "networking" and "fellowship" time. When meetings are held at the office, I have consistently found that the teams do not interact with each other during breaks, and thereby I lose some of the value of the meeting. Unless you are holding your weekly sales meeting with a small group of people, I would always try and book an off-site location. In fact, many companies that we have worked with hold every meeting off-site and report great results. All things considered, probably the only reasons to hold a sales meeting at your office are to save money on expenses, to be closer to information and files you may need during the meeting, and perhaps to make it easier to accommodate meeting participants who are only scheduled to make "cameo" appearances during the meeting. For many meetings, these elements may be a priority.

Off-site Meetings To avoid distractions and accent the importance of the meeting, many managers are choosing to hold even ordinary sales meetings off-site. Almost all hotels and even some country clubs can provide excellent meeting facilities and also fulfill your catering and audiovisual needs. The advantages of working away from the office are that your sales team is together throughout the meeting, they cannot easily run back to their desks, and schedules are easier to maintain. Location is critical, as you will want to align the actual meeting objective with the type of meeting location you choose. If the objective of the meeting is to reward, you may wish to hold the meeting at a country club and perhaps invite spouses to attend. If you have more of a business agenda, the country club environment may be too relaxed, and you may wish to choose a more business-focused hotel. When I first got into the seminar and training industry I remember going to work with client companies who were holding their annual sales meetings in Las Vegas. With so many fun distractions, very few companies could get the participants into their meetings on time, let alone with a clear mind ready to learn. Most companies today only go to the "adult playgrounds" when the objective is to reward top performance. When the meeting agenda calls for education, information, or important business planning, we find the fewer the outside distractions, the better. We have often held our meetings at resort areas in the middle of nowhere because we want 100 percent from the participants. When we began holding our multiday training sessions for the horse trailer manufacturer, we deliberated on whether to hold the events near the factory, which is in a little rural Oklahoma town in a "dry" (no-alcohol) county, or in metropolitan Dallas two hours south. The decision was made to hold the training in the rural town, and it turned out to be the best decision by far. Participants were far from the exciting nightlife of Dallas, and there were no cocktails to liven things up. Study and learning were the only things to do in town, and it has shown in the results. In spite of the grumbling from participants, to this day we still hold those meetings in that small town in rural Oklahoma.

THE NINE-STEP CHECKLIST TO HOLDING GREAT SALES MEETINGS

Here are nine simple ways to make sure that your meetings are different from the rest and your salespeople walk away energized, motivated, and ready to sell. Remember, they will all hold a "meeting" after your meeting and analyze what you have done. Do these nine things and you will always be a hero.

Be Prepared

You need only a little time to prepare if you do it correctly, and the time you spend is always worth it. Make sure you are fully prepared for every meeting. For a typical forty-five-minute sales meeting, the manager should invest two to three hours preparing—the previous week, not the night before. Make sure you arrive at least an hour before the meeting. Arrange the chairs in the room to maximize everyone's attention and minimize distractions. Consider the objective of the meeting when designing the seating arrangements.

Arrange everything else in the room with the same purpose in mind. Audiovisual aids and name tags should be set up in advance. You should have any handouts, on-screen presentations, or reports ready to be distributed to participants. Refreshments should be set up in advance so there are no delays. Decide if you want the coffee service inside your meeting room or outside. I can assure you that if it is in the room, people will get up in the middle of the meeting to refresh their coffee. I recommend lively music as people enter the conference room. It helps establish the mood and gives you a solid starting point to begin the meeting. Your participants will know from the very first moments of the meeting if you have done your homework. I have always found my meetings have been most effective when I have taken time to plan and prepare.

Have an Agenda and Distribute It to Participants Before the Meeting

This might be the best advice I can give you in regards to running more effective meetings. I remember taking a weekly sales meeting that typically took three to four hours and getting it down to forty-five minutes just by preparing an agenda and distributing it to the participants at least twenty-four hours before the meeting. The agenda is your road map. In developing your agenda, ask yourself these four questions:

1. Is it a current topic? Nothing deadens the mind of a participant more than stale material. If this is an overdone topic, perhaps it needs a rest, or at least a new approach.

2. Is the topic relevant to everyone in the group? If there are subjects that pertain to only a few people in the group, perhaps a separate meeting is in order. One of the biggest reasons salespeople claim meetings are a waste of time is that they feel they must sit through topics that are not focused on them, or worse yet, have nothing to do with them. One idea I have used with several companies is to arrange the agenda so that topics are lined up, dealt with, and then the participants who are no longer needed are let go from the meeting to get on with the day. I assure you that those people who have been released will applaud your meeting mastery.

3. Is the topic important? Don't use the big meeting to discuss trivial subjects. Also remember that if it can be covered in writing, you should do so and give the meeting time to more important matters.

4. Is your presentation upbeat? Make sure you keep things moving and moving in a positive direction. Consider your topic and how you can present it in the most exciting manner.

Start On Time and End On Time, or Sooner!

Respect your participants' time by starting and ending punctually. Make sure everyone knows that it is inappropriate to be late for any meeting you call. In fact, I recommend a system to fine people who show up late. Perhaps the person showing up late must bring bagels or special coffee to the next meeting. You could also set up a charity for the tardy folks to contribute to or have them donate to the year-end company party. Any of these ideas can be effective; the critical element is to make sure that everyone knows, and that they know up front. Many managers enable the tardy participant by conducting a quick recap of what has been discussed. If there are people who are rude enough to be late, they miss what has been covered. Period! By reviewing the meeting in the middle, not only do you "teach" these salespeople that being late is somewhat acceptable, but you waste everyone else's time during the review. Be known as someone who starts on time and, in order to respect everyone's time, someone who doesn't accept lateness. You might also want to assign a neutral party to act as moderator to keep the clock and bring it to everyone's attention when the meeting starts to fall behind schedule.

Have Fewer but Better Meetings

Call a meeting only when it is absolutely necessary. When you do call a meeting, make sure it is a good one. If whatever you need to communicate can be done via e-mail or written memoranda, then do just that. Once every so often, cancel a meeting well in advance and cite that the reason is there is nothing that needs to be discussed and no reason to meet. You will really begin to earn the respect of your team on that call. One thing I have done on occasion, when I have a meeting scheduled, people are already in the office, and there is nothing too significant that needs to be covered, is to call a quick stand-up meeting. Remove all the chairs from the conference room. People will have the strangest looks on their faces when they come in and there is nowhere to sit. Announce that the agenda is brief, and you are going to meet standing up. I assure you that it could be one of the most efficient meetings ever, as people will be uncomfortable standing and will get right to the point.

Include, Don't Exclude

Invite only the people you need at the meeting, but do not forget to include members of the company who may have insight or provide valuable knowledge. Most sales managers routinely meet only with their salespeople, but consider inviting the other members of the team in as we have discussed before. One idea that I have successfully used is to have members of the firm from other departments come in to discuss a "day in the life" in their role at the company. It is amazing how much more cooperation and efficiency we get when everyone understands the different responsibilities and jobs people perform.

Whenever Possible, Bring In a Guest Speaker

I have found that one of the most powerful things you can do to reinforce your message is to bring in a guest speaker. I mentioned this in another chapter, but just think of the power you will have by having someone else come in and address your team and support you, the manager, as well as the company. The guest speaker can be from outside or inside the company, but your meetings will be a great deal more energizing if different people are taking the podium, keeping things lively. Obviously this makes your job easier as well. However, I strongly recommend that you never allow anyone to speak to your sales team until you have met with the speaker, discussed the presentation, and made sure you have asked the speaker to help support your program as well.

Maintain the Focus of the Meeting and Stick to the Agenda

Do whatever it takes to keep your meetings on topic at all times. Business topics can be a little stale at times, and many managers will open the meeting talking about last night's big game or the latest movie. These digressions can sometimes go on for a great deal of time, and then, as if all of a sudden, you are twenty minutes into the meeting. One of the reasons these conversations start in the first place is often because you decide not to get started on the agenda while you are waiting for people who are late, thus teaching those people that they don't need to be on time. Keep the focus, start on time, and finish early, and then you can talk about the social stuff with all who wish to participate, without holding others hostage.

Capture Action Items

Make sure you have planned a system to capture, summarize, and delegate key action items from every meeting. Whether you simply write them down, use large flip-chart pages that stick to the wall, or use a high-tech scanning electronic whiteboard, get the action items in writing. By taking time to capture the essential items, summarize the notes, and then perhaps even distribute them via e-mail to the participants, you eliminate the age-old question "What did we accomplish at that meeting?"

Get Input and Feedback from the Participants

Getting feedback is a great way to measure the effectiveness of your meetings. Not only will you learn what you did right, but you will also uncover what can be improved. Ask for open and honest feedback. Make it anonymous through written evaluations if necessary, but reflect and review how each meeting went. In this manner you will continue to grow and make your meetings even more effective.

HOW TO DELIVER AN
EFFECTIVE PRESENTATION

Once you get the details arranged, the agenda established, and the participants assembled and waiting, what happens next? That's right, you're on! President Franklin Delano Roosevelt had some great advice for speakers and presenters: "Be sincere, be brief and be seated!" I think you should also be prepared and be yourself.

Everyone dreads bombing at the podium. The fear is understandable; for many managers and executives, their career advancement can be determined by their ability to speak and inspire an audience. The people you manage are watching, and it can be a challenge, especially when you consider that you often have to address the same group week after week. As I travel the country giving seminars on sales and sales management, I find that it is much easier to speak to new audiences than it is to speak to my own sales team. For a set meeting, the preparation and design of the presentation is that much more critical. Most sales managers are not professional speakers, but many professional speakers started out as sales managers, and running weekly sales meetings can be a great training ground to develop your public speaking skills.

The following are some excellent tips on speaking before an audience:

- Know what you are going to say and practice it until you are comfortable.
- Research your material. Be prepared to answer questions beyond the scope of your talk.
- Include anecdotes and personal examples.
- Pause and take a breath before beginning. It is not necessary to start rattling off your message the moment you hit the front of the room.

- Don't read your message, deliver it!
- It is almost impossible to talk too loudly, so make sure you use your voice to deliver the full impact of the message.
- Maintain eye contact; do not just look at your notes.
- Sit down when you are finished.
- Conviction and passion are powerful allies. If you are "sold" the sincerity will come through. This is especially important if you are delivering a message from above and your bosses have assigned you the task of giving the news.
- Don't try and force an unnatural style that does not reflect your personality. The audience will recognize the strain. If you are not naturally a joke teller, don't feel you need to be telling jokes just because you are at the podium. You should also understand the difference between comedy and humor. Comedy requires a special delivery or timing to make it funny, while humor is funny even if it is in writing. Unless you are really good at delivering comedy, stay with humor and you can't go wrong. Of course, it is not necessary for you to start the meeting with some kind of joke. Use an attention-getter and opening questions instead.
- Be brief and to the point. Nothing loses the attention of an audience like a speech that runs on and on unnecessarily.
- Use language the listeners will understand. There is no need to show off your vocabulary.
- Stay relaxed throughout the meeting. You will appear more friendly and credible.

- Be sure to talk with your team and not at them. A good sales meeting has the tone of a discussion instead of a lecture.
- Always expect the unexpected. There is usually some form of distraction or another at every meeting. The best way to keep attention is to walk away from a distraction instead of walking towards it. In other words, if a water pitcher falls on the ground, do not walk over to pick it up, but rather walk away from the incident to draw your participants' attention. I would not even mention it unless there is some chance for comic relief. If the distraction is unavoidable, you can also use it as an opportunity to have fun and endear yourself to your audience. I was recently in Oklahoma City, giving a presentation in the convention center. In the next room another meeting was getting started. All of a sudden, in the middle of my presentation, a loud, booming rendition of "The Star-Spangled Banner" came on. It was so loud I could not talk over it, and I had no choice but to ask everyone to stand and join in! It was hilarious and created a very memorable moment.
- Finally, plan a powerful close that includes an inspirational challenge and a quick word of appreciation, such as, "We can do this. We have a strong team. I enjoy working with all of you, and you make my job easier. Thank you. Now, let's go make something happen!"

Follow these tips and I am confident you will give excellent presentations. If you still feel nervous about getting up in front of a group, then I recommend that you join a group where you can practice. The Toastmasters International organization would be an excellent resource. You should also consider attending the Dale Carnegie Human Relations course. They call it "the Dale course," and it is an excellent opportunity to practice your speaking skills.

TELECONFERENCES AND WEB-BASED CONFERENCES

Many companies are keeping their sales teams out of the office altogether. With technology and higher-bandwidth connections, there are fewer and fewer weekly sales meetings conducted in the traditional way. There are also many home-based sales forces that may have an annual national sales meeting, but the weekly in-person gathering has become impractical.

I feel the loss of traditional meetings is regrettable because the manager can learn so much about what is really happening when the sales team gathers in person. In-person sales meetings are also great opportunities to build teamwork and interpersonal relationships, two important intangible assets quickly slipping away from today's sales forces.

Managers who are not able to meet with their sales teams as often as they like should consider a teleconference or Web-based conference. While it is not a total substitute for a more traditional sales meeting, it is a good stopgap measure to keep in touch. Having said that, there are certain instances when a "virtual sales meeting" can be the best call that a manager can make.

FIVE INSTANCES WHEN A VIRTUAL SALES MEETING IS A GOOD CALL

- When important information must be relayed fast and sending an e-mail or voicemail may be too impersonal or be misconstrued
- When there is an emergency or challenge that requires interaction and time is of the essence
- When misinformation about the company or product needs to be corrected fast
- When the manager needs up-to-date intelligence from the field
- When company policies change

Making a Virtual Conference a Success

There are specific things you can do to make your teleconference or Web-based meeting a success. Here is a checklist to help you get the most from your meeting:

- Set up the agenda like you would any meeting. Be aware of time zone changes when you schedule the time and date. Get the agenda out in advance.
- Make sure everyone is aware that their complete attention is required. One of the biggest challenges when holding these types of virtual meetings is that participants tend to multitask and get distracted easily. Unless it's absolutely necessary, they should not be on a wireless phone, especially driving down the freeway! I have had salespeople try and participate in a conference call on their cell phones with the top down

on their cars. All that the rest of us heard was the howling wind. If you are holding a Web conference, make sure the participants close their Internet browsers and e-mail organizers. No surfing on your time is allowed.

- Inform everyone that they will be expected to participate actively. No heavy breathers! You will want to constantly ask direct questions of participants, such as "Dennis, what do you think of that idea?" Once the rest of the participants know you will be calling people out, they will pay more attention.

- Make sure that people calling from home have established a "quiet zone" and understand how to use the mute button on their phones. It is extremely annoying to try to hold a business conference with dogs barking in the background.

- Establish a good phone bridge service. There are many vendors who can provide this type of phone or Web service. If you cannot find one, then just open up any Internet search engine and do a search under Web or phone conferencing. You will find plenty of options. You also want to make sure everyone on a Web conference has the same connection speed so the conference can proceed smoothly. If you have pictures, diagrams, or charts that are being discussed and one person is on a dial-up connection, the whole meeting has to wait on the slowest link.

- Act as a referee and help sort out the conversation if several of your participants speak out at once. Be aware of those people who talk just to hear themselves speak.

- Make sure everyone is heard. You may need to even draw out some people to get their opinions, since you will not be able to read body language on the phone or through a Web camera. For instance, "Diane, what do you think of Joe's suggested course of action?"

- Don't make any rushed decisions unless you are convinced you are doing the right thing. Because of the speed at which these conferences happen, sometimes we get pushed into the wrong course of action too quickly.
- Commit to some action, even if it is only to review what has been said. Your team will want to feel the conference has some positive effect. Obtain commitments from the participants as well.
- Send out a written summary of the call. You will have taken notes, I am sure, and you may also want to record the call. Most conference services will provide that service for a small extra fee, and it is quite handy to have a full recording of all that was said for later reference.

YOUR DEFINING MOMENT AS A SALES MANAGER

Every profession has a defining moment in which the world can see whether you are truly a professional or just an amateur. It only takes listening to a few bars of a song when a singer begins to tell whether the person is any good at singing. Just watch the first swings of the day and you can probably guess within a few strokes what a golfer's handicap is likely to be.

In the past twenty-five years I have seen thousands of sales meetings, conducted by managers throughout the world. I can tell within a few short minutes whether a sales manager is a professional or an amateur just by how he or she begins a sales meeting. I would bet you can too. Of all the things you do as a sales manager, nothing else is immediately seen by everyone in your company and anyone else who's watching. As an effective leading sales manager, this is an area you want to excel in.

SALES MEETING CHECKLIST

After each meeting you conduct, take a few minutes and ask yourself these questions to review what happened and how you can grow as a meeting leader.

- Was I really prepared, or was I "winging it"?
- Did I start the meeting on time?
- Did the participants respond freely and easily to my questions?
- Did I keep the meeting on track? Did we stay focused?
- Did I refrain from lecturing or playing the expert?
- Did I maintain healthy control of the meeting?
- Were distractions handled properly?
- Did I keep the interest of the participants?
- Did I make full use of the audiovisual tools?
- Were the points covered thoroughly?
- Did I handle questions properly?
- Did the majority of the participants enjoy the meeting?
- Did I give them something to think about?
- Did I end the meeting on time?
- Did I learn something? If so, what?

SUMMARY

There is perhaps no quicker way to influence or motivate a sales team to greater performance than through properly held sales meetings. And, there is probably no quicker way to de-motivate a sales team than through an improperly held sales meeting. Prepare thoroughly, make sure you have the right people, create and distribute an agenda, stay focused and time-conscious, and get feedback from the participants. Practice and be comfortable with your presentations—this is no time to wing it. Make sure you are ready and have followed the checklists. By following the guidelines in this chapter, you should be well on your way to running great sales meetings that inspire and lift up your team.

6

When you bring new salespeople to the team, it's important to get them promptly to the point where they can perform effectively on their own. In this chapter, that process will be outlined. Obviously, training and motivation bring value to the workforce. They should be at the top of every firm's agenda. Growing—and even surviving—demands constant effort to improve the selling competency of your sales team.

What sets the profession of selling apart from all other occupations is the extent to which frustration and rejection are integral parts of it. Unlike other positions, selling requires its practitioners to deal with rejection every working day. A salesperson may also have to deal with issues not directly involved in closing the sale. These issues include such potentials for trouble and frustration as credit approval, billing, delivery, installation, and follow-through. Usually most or all of these requirements are met by people in other departments. Nevertheless, customers tend to hold salespeople responsible for things over which they may have little or no organizational control. In many companies, successful salespeople must not only be skilled in sales, but

also possess diplomatic skills strong enough to gain the cooperation of other departments. Thus the salesperson personality
is unique, and requires a different sort of management. We call
the necessary vision and implementation of sales management
motivation and counseling.

One of the things we have learned about motivating salespeople
is that when you try to motivate the individual salesperson you
will constantly be frustrated. Individual salespeople are motivated
by so many different things and in so many different ways that
to focus on individuals would be like herding cats. It's more
effective to work at creating a motivating environment. Once you
are making progress toward providing a motivating environment,
start working on upgrading your sales team. Recruit and develop
people who will become motivated within your motivation-
enhanced environment. In this manner, management can control
the environment for the sales team as a whole rather than chasing
around the individuals. As you pursue this plan, the entire team
you currently have may not fit into the ideal environment you're
creating. As a result, you may need to go through some turnover in
order to make this cultural change.

In this section, we use a case study to get you thinking about
how to interact with your salespeople in the areas of motivation
and counseling. You may have already dealt with this situation;
maybe you dealt with it appropriately and helped the salesperson
regain his or her usual productivity. Maybe you didn't, and lost
the salesperson.

TRY THIS CASE SNAPSHOT

Diana has been a salesperson with your company for nearly a year
now. She was quite active in the beginning and had some pretty
decent sales numbers. You were excited about having her on your

team because she really looked like the next heavy-hitting sales champion. But lately it seems that she has lost her enthusiasm for the business. Her sales numbers have dipped and she does not seem to be maintaining the prospecting activity you recommend. Her attendance at your weekly sales meetings has been sporadic; when Diana does show up she comes in late.

When you speak to her, you get excuses and empty promises to attend the next meeting. You know that Diana used to like the business and needs to earn the money. How will you remotivate her and get her back into the business with the enthusiasm she had initially?

I have used this example many times in seminars and custom training, and invariably managers tell me the first thing is to discover what's going on with Diana; specifically, what triggered her change of attitude.

"Find out what's wrong with Diana," is the way many managers put it. When they face a real-life situation of this kind, managers who take that attitude often get frustrated because they can't get to the heart of the matter.

The reason for their frustration can be something as simple as the difference between saying to Diana, "What's wrong with you?" instead of, "What's troubling you, Diana?" It's far more than a mere choice of wrong terminology; it's taking the attitude that the salesperson is at fault. Naturally the salesperson feels attacked and gets defensive, even hostile.

Most salespeople know when they are not performing to their potential, or when they are in a slump. Indeed, how can they *not* know? When you approach them, even with the best of intentions to help them, you risk shutting them down. Communication may come to a crashing halt before you get a bit of useful information or a single insight. Thus you won't be able to get to the root of the issue and find a way to move past it.

In this case study, Diana could be going through any number of challenges, some of which may be too personal and emotionally overwhelming for her to discuss. If married, her marriage may be in trouble; if single, she may have some other romantic complication. She could be having problems with her kids, or be facing serious health issues. The list is endless.

Here's what I have learned as a leader. When I approach salespeople in Diana's situation from the perspective of finding out what's wrong with them, often they won't cooperate. Without the information needed to work through the problem, I'm stalemated.

However, if I start with *me* and approach them from an angle that's less intrusive into private emotional concerns, I often get more voluntary cooperation. When faced with this situation, you might say something like this:

"Diana, we had a commitment that we agreed upon when you joined the team. I agreed to do some things to better manage you and you agreed to do certain things. You know I schedule time to review our mutual commitments. I feel like I was following through on those commitments, but maybe I'm missing an area. Obviously, the production is not happening; we are not achieving these goals.

"As a leader, I'm wondering whether there is anything I could be doing better to help you achieve the goals? What am I not doing for you?"

Nine times out of ten, they will say, "Oh no, it's not you, I am going through . . ." and drop an illuminating hint or even go into detail about what's holding them back. Maybe the original goals aren't important to Diana anymore, and we need to reassess the goals. So the key to overcoming situations in which salespeople are having problems is to spend time with them. This may involve getting back into the field with them again; you may need to reevaluate the goals. Approach this challenge with you as the focus, not them. You will get better results in most cases.

The movie *Glengarry Glen Ross* shows an extreme example in which the bigwig manager, played by Alec Baldwin, visits the local office to "motivate" its salespeople for the monthly sales contest. Baldwin's character confuses motivation with intimidation. He announces the incentives this way: "The good news is you're fired, the bad news is, you've got—all you've got—is just one week to regain your job starting with tonight. Oh, have I got your attention now? Good, because we're adding a little something to this month's sales contest. As you all know, first prize is a Cadillac El Dorado. Anybody want to see the second prize? It's a set of steak knives. Third prize, you're fired. You get the picture, are you laughing now? You've got leads. Mitch and Murray paid good money to get those names so you could sell them. If you can't close the leads you've been given, you can't close @%#&."

Perhaps you've been on the receiving end of the intimidation system of sales management; if so, you may have witnessed the result. The strongest salespeople took their highly sought-after skills where they would be treated with respect. Who remained? The poorest performers who felt they had no choice. Thus the average sales competency of the sales force dropped like a stone. What happened to sales volume in the absence of the top performers? You tell me.

Anything that smacks of intimidation is risky in today's society. Clearly, it's not the most effective way to motivate salespeople.

EIGHT STEPS TO A MOTIVATED SALES ORGANIZATION

1. Set the Example with Your Attitude

I like to think of myself not only as the CEO of my company, but also as the CAO, the chief attitude officer. What I bring to the table each and every day has an impact on how the team responds. If your attitude is bad, you don't want to bring that into your interaction with your salespeople. Don't share it with them. You can assume 80 percent of the people you gripe to don't care, and the other 20 percent are happy to hear that you're more messed up than they are. If things are going poorly for you, take a moment before you go into the office to put your woes on hold until the end of the day. Always focus on the positive before you walk into the office.

As a leader you will find, if you haven't already, that if you give the team an excuse they will run with it for all it's worth. If you let them conclude—or even suspect—that you think the market is down, the economy is slumping, the product is bad, or whatever, they will exploit your indiscretion to the max. Attitude is a big part of strong sales performance. Think of yourself as the pilot of a small plane carrying three passengers flying into serious turbulence. If you show fear or even a little concern, your passengers will panic. But no matter how severely your airplane gets tossed around, if you tell them, "This is nothing; I've been through a lot worse in this plane," they will stay reasonably calm.

In the same way, you have to set the appropriate example for your salespeople. If you want a confident sales force, you have to exude confidence; if you want enthusiastic salespeople, you have to be enthusiastic. If you are on fire with enthusiasm, people will drive for miles to watch you burn!

Some people are naturally enthusiastic and excited. They don't need a snooze alarm; they jump out of bed, gobble their breakfasts, and run out the door. They can't wait to start their days and see what's in store. The challenge with this group is that about 90 percent of them are under the age of five. You can learn a lot about attitude from your children, or from the children you know.

With my involvement with my three sons' Little League teams, I see examples of this kind of enthusiasm all the time. For several summers, the two older boys have played in traveling tournaments lasting up to a week. So all the parents plan the travel, take time off from work, and spend a ton of money getting everyone to these out-of-town games. It's a big commitment.

One year my son Randy's tournament was out of state. In the first game—boom—we lose. Then the second game—boom—we lose again. All the parents were at the ball field, and as soon as the umpire yelled, "You're outta there!" the parents were all complaining, whining, and boo-hooing. And what were the kids doing? They were shouting, "Where's the pool?" "When's lunch?"

As soon as the game was over, they were like, "Let's go; move on, man; we're done; that was cool, but let's go have fun!"

So if you can create a more childlike environment in your office, everyone will have a lot of fun at work. Notice that I didn't say *childish* environment. There's a world of difference between *childlike* and *childish*. Make sure you establish the difference.

You have to be the leader of the attitude. Our attitude and leadership was suddenly and severely tested on September 11, 2001. I had an interesting experience on that tragic day while we were putting on a Tom Hopkins seminar in Honolulu, Hawaii.

If it had been anywhere in the continental United States, it wouldn't have happened. After being awakened by news of the tragedy, we met that morning and decided to go forward with the event and handle it the best way we could. Leadership was going to be the key that day. If we had been closer to New York, no one would have showed up, but the people of Honolulu did come. Back in my office in Scottsdale, Arizona, no one was working. They were all glued to the news on television. There was nothing else to do; customers and prospects were in no mood to take calls. No work was done for several days.

As a leader, you have a choice. President Bush encouraged us to go on, to keep moving forward, and to get back to our daily routines. If you have established good leadership, you can make that happen for the betterment of all.

Of course you want to grieve and honor those who lost their lives; you feel a deep sense of compassion for their families; and you are outraged at the brutality of the terrorists—attitudes that come from the heart. We must never forget September 11, but at some point we must get on with our lives. If you had allowed your team to use September 11 as an excuse, they could have drawn out poor production for six months.

2. Be Consistent in Your Leadership

As I travel for Tom Hopkins and Results Seminars, I get the unique opportunity to lead training seminars for Tom's company and many others. As part of my training course, I will never take on an assignment without spending time with the sales team, riding along to appointments, sitting in on appointments, seeing them in action and customizing the Tom Hopkins material to that company and industry. When I spend time with the salespeople, I get to learn what they think, and how they feel and respond. One observation I have noticed is that they would rather have you, the sales manager, be a jerk all the time than to never know when you are going to be one. Inconsistency—never knowing when the other shoe will drop—is a powerful *de*motivator.

3. Treat Each Salesperson's Needs Individually

One of the worst things you can ever do is make a salesperson feel like a number to the company, or just another steer in the cattle car. I have seen very good salespeople leave companies for this precise reason. When the company has an open attitude that if you can't do the job, someone else will, salespeople begin to feel unimportant and then they don't do their jobs well.

4. Make High-Quality Training Materials Available

Have a library of resources that includes several authors and categories: sales training, motivational material, goal-setting ideas, time-management strategies, and so on.

To use the example of kids again, my oldest son, Scott, pitches for his baseball team. I used to pitch in school and I know the general mechanics of how to pitch. When he was about twelve I tried to coach him about not stepping too far back off the rubber. Stepping back causes you to go off balance and you throw from your ear like a catcher instead of extending your arm back to get more velocity. Do you think Scott would listen to me? No.

So I hired a coach, a retired major league pitcher who lived in Scottsdale, to be Scott's pitching coach at $50 an hour. He took one look at Scott and said, "You're stepping too far off the rubber, you're off balance, and you're throwing like a catcher from the ear instead of extending back." Guess what Scott starts to do? Follow the direction! I laugh to myself that I had to pay $50 to have an outsider tell my son what he needed to do, because Scott wouldn't listen to me. I was too close to the situation.

Having a good variety of tools in your training library will allow you to go to the appropriate topic for any situation. If it's a time-management issue, you can pull out *Time Management Training* and agree to talk about it after *x* number of days. Giving people a chance to delve into the subject before it's raised in a meeting tends to encourage discussion about the issue.

Here's a good tip about checking in on the personal growth of your salespeople. When you give someone a book to read, go into the book about one third of the way, and find a margin to write something like, "Hope this is helping. When you get to this point, contact me, and I will take you to lunch and we will discuss the book!" Don't tell them it's there. A couple of weeks later, ask them if they are enjoying the book or if they finished it. If they talk about how great it was, but have never asked you for a free lunch, you know they never invested the time to read it! A lot of people will pay you lip service, but will never follow through.

A last thought on the importance of training materials: I never went to college. I intended to when I moved to Arizona with my mom after I graduated from high school in Illinois. Like many people I started to work, but unlike many people I got lucky with the opportunities that came to me. I got placed in the midst of the sales-training industry when I started with Tom Hopkins, and the philosophy was practice what you preach, so I had exposure to lots of training and resources. I read everything I could get my hands on, I agreed with some of it, didn't agree with some of it, but I learned a great deal—not just sales training, but management ideas, time management, goal setting, business techniques, and even many personal interests. Training materials gave me the education I missed as I worked my way through the sales industry, and they can help you and your employees in the same way.

5. Provide Plentiful Opportunities to Be Recognized

I have covered this in depth in other parts of this book. But here in this convenient location are two additional tips for giving lots of opportunities for recognition, and doing so within a busy schedule.

1. The tools of technology, such as e-mail and voice mail can help you expedite the recognition process and will mean a lot to your salespeople and other staff. When I'm traveling, I often pick up the cell phone during a late-night/early-morning layover when the time zones favor calling, or I type out several e-mail messages on the plane to send on my next e-mail connection.

The messages say something like, "Hey, thanks for being on our team. I know I don't say it enough, but you provide real value in achieving the company goals. We really appreciate what you do." When they get to work the next morning the message is waiting. It's a great way to help someone start the day. I've heard directly from people who have received one of these messages, or from one of their coworker friends, that such a message turned the recipient's attitude around. This is especially effective for someone who is a bit down that morning; perhaps the normal rejection involved in sales is getting to him or her. If your message goes to someone who is flying high, it spurs him or her to fly even higher.

Either way, you boost productivity and take a big step toward retaining your strongest salespeople at little or no cost. Doing this only requires you to invest some otherwise nonproductive time.

2. Plaques and certificates provide good keepsakes for employees to remind them of their accomplishments and the recognition given them. You will find more detailed information in this chapter under "Sales Contests and Incentives." An attractive plaque will probably be displayed in the recipient's den, where it will be a source of pride to the owner.

6. Work Together to Set Goals

Very few managers collaborate when setting goals, but effective leaders live by this. Companies give one of their paramount management controls different names: budget, quota, goals by territory, management by objective (MBO)—but they all amount to the same thing. We'll call it the quota, or goal.

In traditional top-down companies, information flows only one way. Top-down companies always generate quotas at corporate headquarters for the company's salespeople. Often these corporate-generated quotas are based on wishful thinking, or on top management's need to show growth. Many times these fantasyland quotas from the top drop with a humongous thud on the branch sales managers.

The task of the branch sales managers is to hand these often-unrealistic quotas to the salespeople to execute in their territories. However, none of the salespeople had any input on setting their quotas. How much buy-in to such goals will the salespeople have? Maybe none. So what we have learned is to work with each salesperson and set the goal together. Sometimes we have to raise their sights; sometimes we have to lower their sights without crushing their vision. The point is, we adjust the goal to meet the company goals, but give the salesperson involved an opportunity to discuss it and agree with it so they buy into the goal and *the* vision becomes *their* vision.

Top-down managements say, in effect, "Here's what you've got to accomplish, or else." What happens if you hand down such a directive? You will lose good people, often your best. Many salespeople experience this rough treatment; most react negatively.

Often it happens like this: Managers casually ask their salespeople what they think they can do in the coming year. Most salespeople will give an estimate based on what they accomplished the year before and the growth they perceive in their territory. Assuming no change in the size or composition of the territory, the answers to some or all of several other questions may need to be taken into account in order to come up with a realistic forecast:

- Is the territory's economy prospering or have serious downturns occurred? For example, have any large companies shut down a plant or moved their headquarters elsewhere? Even if your salespeople weren't selling directly to the departed companies, the loss of their local purchases and jobs will depress many small businesses in the territory who may be your industry's best prospects. Conversely, if some large companies moved in, the territory may offer expanded opportunities to the salesperson.

- What effect will whatever changes that have occurred in the national economy have on your industry?
- Are new competitors gaining a foothold?
- How do your products or services stack up against new developments among your existing competitors?

In a perfect world considerations such as these would be carefully analyzed before a sales goal or quota is decided upon. Since such analyses take time and require information that may not be available, managements often base their forecasts on wishful thinking.

In those cases, when the quotas come out, they will often be larger numbers than many salespeople believe are reachable. When such quotas are accompanied by the policy statement "Achieve it or be terminated," some of the sales team's best producers are likely to start sending out their résumés. And rightfully so. After being denied any opportunity to influence their quotas, few salespeople will buy into goals set by people far removed from the territory in question. Managements who thus show a lack of interest in and respect for the salespeople's opinion of their own territory's potential have only themselves to blame when their salespeople feel insulted and outraged enough to resign. Whether or not the goals handed down from on high are achievable doesn't matter if the salespeople never buy into it. As a result, motivation and company loyalty take a heavy beating. This happens a lot in the companies I work with.

Salespeople sometimes feel their company is greedy and uses its salespeople exclusively to fulfill the manager's goals, not their own. Prevent this attitude from becoming a serious demotivator; work with your salespeople on setting goals for their territories— within reason, of course. Listen to their input.

Occasionally, some individuals will try for a low quota so they won't have to work very hard. Most well-trained salespeople know what the limitations are in their territories and will tell you when asked. If you want to confirm their estimates, learn what is realistic by putting in some windshield time with them. When salespeople have solid input into their quotas, they will attack their work with maximum energy because they feel they own their goals.

7. Hold Planned and Organized Meetings

This is huge. It is a big demotivator if done incorrectly. Let's say you're attending a Tom Hopkins seminar or one of my Management Seminars. To get to it, you had to travel some distance.

I opened the meeting by saying, "Good morning. Thanks for coming. Sorry, but I don't really have a lot of things planned. We're going to talk about some management stuff, and maybe you'll have some questions." You'd feel like I had totally wasted your time. I didn't honor your time. As we all know, time is not subject to refund; once spent it's gone forever.

We place enormous value on our attendees' time. When we stage a seminar, we put together a workbook, make room arrangements, develop a PowerPoint presentation, and prepare a timeline to follow. We make sure we have planned out the event to use the time wisely so that when you walk out at the end of the day, you will feel it was a good use of your time.

Many sales departments across the United States hold that weekly meeting without any direction and it goes on for a couple of hours, as these blunder meetings usually do. When the salespeople are finally able to get out of there, they hold smaller meetings around the water cooler talking about what a waste of time the first meeting was. They pick it apart, trying to rebuild their enthusiasm, which took a heavy hit in the blunder meeting.

A useful example comes from my work with a large manufacturing company. Their weekly Wednesday conference call was about three hours long, and most people felt it wasted everybody's time. We decided that we needed to make the 'meeting' worthwhile, so the first thing we did was develop a conference call agenda. It was posted via e-mail on Tuesday. If a topic wasn't on that week's agenda it didn't get discussed. We put the production issues up front, so when we were finished with those topics the production staff could go on with their day and not waste their time sitting through sales issues. If something needed to be discussed, they had to have the topic to me by Monday to get it on the agenda. We took that three-hour call down to between forty-five minutes and an hour. People felt that it was a good use of their time. The result? The company got a significant but cost-free boost in productivity.

Organize all your meetings. It requires effort, so organizing meetings must be given high priority. Careful planning and follow-through is also vital for extracurricular company events, like picnics and incentive trips, especially if families will be included. If your salespeople earn an annual trip and will be required to attend certain events or training, get them an agenda *early*. People like to know what to expect, particularly when traveling, and even more so when their families accompany them. Not having an agenda for weekly events or major events is annoying. Your salespeople will come better prepared when they have a copy of the agenda well in advance.

8. Conduct Regularly Scheduled Performance Reviews

Most salespeople don't get enough performance reviews, and many companies shy away from doing them. Why? Traditionally, salespeople and employees in general expect a raise when they get reviewed. In our group, we have separated performance reviews and merit increases entirely. We tell people from day one that consideration of these two issues will not coincide. Typically, if they don't think they have gotten a good enough raise, or none at all, they are not going to listen to what you have to say in the performance review, good or bad, and they will get disgruntled. If the raise is not big enough when the review was spectacular, they feel their performance really isn't that good in their manager's opinion. This will raise issues in future performance.

We do cost-of-living adjustments, but we don't do merit increases. The team bonus rewards increased production and the achievement of goals. You can easily merit-increase your sales force out of the industry-standard salary for that position. If they stay long enough they will be making more working for you than they could anywhere else. If they get too comfortable, it can be dangerous.

With salespeople, you should do performance reviews more often than once a year. You have to let people know where they stand and what kind of a job they are doing, whether it's outstanding or needs more effort. Many of us in management think that if the salespeople are making a good fee-for-service income, then they are convinced that they doing well. If they aren't, then they know they aren't doing well and will probably leave your company anyway. With our inside team we conduct performance reviews every thirty days; with our outside team we conduct them every ninety days. We look at the goals that were set and how they fit into the company goals, and then look at their Position Results Description.

I had an experience with one company that conducted performance reviews with its salespeople once a year, and tied them into an annual merit increase or no increase in some cases. As a result, the salespeople got lethargic or lost motivation halfway through the year, if not sooner. Bad plan. There was no consistent or regular incentive for salespeople who had no clear picture of how their performance was being evaluated.

I always start with the notion that people are their own worst critic and ask, "How do you think you're doing?" I get them to start talking and most of the time they bring up the same issues I had planned to discuss, so I have some thoughts prepared on how to work with those challenges.

"How can I do a better job to help you?" I ask, and always end the review on a positive note with a plan of action for the things we will work on or focus on in the next x number of days, weeks, or months.

I have found doing the reviews every thirty days with the inside team has been very proactive and gives us the ability to correct behavioral challenges promptly. The inside team has a high-activity job, and their Position Results Descriptions are set up so that if their production goals are being met, we don't care about activity. Maybe we want them to do a hundred calls a day, but if the production is on track, I don't care if it took only sixty-eight calls a day to get there.

In the reverse, if their production goals are not being met, we pull the call logs and look at the activity. Sometimes it helps us see patterns. If the other inside representatives look to the team leader to make the day's first call, and that person does nothing but drink coffee for the first forty-five minutes of the day, the rest of the group will do the same. With frequent reviews, we can redirect such behavior sooner rather than later. Reviews will help you solve challenges and/or encourage good habits in a one-on-one environment.

I think the team finds value in it as well, because they know that once a month or quarter they get a chance to check in with us, and to solve issues bothering them about clients or other members of the team. Having frequent, assured private meetings with each member of the team also postpones some of those issues to the appropriate scheduled time, instead of burdening the team member with frequent interruptions of the "Hey, do you have a minute?" ilk.

All reviews should be done professionally and face-to-face whenever possible. If you have salespeople local to your offices, conduct reviews in person, not over the phone. If you have out-of-town representatives, reviews will need to be conducted over the phone. For legal reasons, it's always wise to have a third person present when reviewing someone of the opposite sex.

These eight steps will help you create motivating environments. But keep the reality of motivation in mind: Sometimes you simply can't motivate someone else. This might come as a surprise since I've just given you a program of steps to do that very thing. But sometimes it won't work. You may not be able motivate another person, but you can and must create an environment that will encourage people to be motivated. I try to work on the environment, and if people can't motivate themselves, they may not be a good fit for either my company or your organization.

Motivation is like a bath; you need it every day. I had a very successful outside representative by the name of David, who always used to say, "Motivation is like Chinese food—after you've had it, you are hungry for it again in a couple of hours."

A MANAGER'S DUTY WHEN A STRONG SALESPERSON SLUMPS

I have seen some very successful salespeople fall into a slump and climb out again on their own. Others, equally successful, go through difficult slumps if they feel their managers are unapproachable or unavailable to help them—and the slump gets worse. This is unfortunate, because a manager needs to lead the slumper's group in helping the person get back on track. Many in the group will act as though assisting a quality salesperson, someone who usually provides a full share of value to the team, is an inconvenience. It's the manager's responsibility to see that a once-promising but still salvageable salesperson does not continue going south. That would mean that he or she would eventually leave or be let go simply because the original commitment between the two parties was not clear.

The Salesperson's Review and Performance Appraisal

Being reviewed is most stressful to people who know their production hasn't met the goals. They may be afraid they're about to be fired; at the least, they fear they're in for an unpleasant meeting, if not a humiliating chew-out. So their attitude when they come in is likely to be fearful, defensive, even hostile. In the grip of such feelings, it's hard for them to absorb constructive suggestions.

So your first need is to ease their stress, relieve their fears, and help them get into a positive frame of mind so they can and will take your helpful suggestions to heart. This assumes that your intention is to bring the people being reviewed up to speed. This means you believe they can be salvaged. If not, your purpose is to build a file to support dismissal. Our discussion here applies to the former case, salespeople you believe can become effective members of your team.

Bear in mind that your method of handling reviews will have a strong effect on whether your sales team develops a powerful emotional desire to win your approval and help you achieve your goals. Such a desire is based on personal respect, and on the belief that you can be depended on to do everything you can to boost their self-esteem and help them achieve their goals, and in the process, help you achieve yours. Do you truly believe your salespeople must be driven, and that hard driving and heavy pressure is the most reliable way to increase production? This usually means you will intimidate and humiliate nonperformers. If so, be aware that such actions spread discord and even hatred among your sales force. In such an environment, teamwork won't flourish and enthusiasm withers.

The time when the best class of salespeople could be driven by fear passed into history when the Great Depression ended. That's how far out of date you are if you're still relying on heavy-handed tactics to spur sales. Today calls for *leadership*. Exploit every opportunity you can find to demonstrate that you lead from the front with enthusiasm, confidence, and ideas, rather than driving from behind with nothing but the whip.

When handled with warm regard for the sensitivities of those being reviewed, the review is a priceless opportunity to enhance your personal standing, strengthen team spirit, and build sales. Here's a checklist for gaining maximum results from performance appraisals:

The Nine-Point Checklist for Gaining Maximum Results from Performance Appraisals

1. Begin by complimenting the salesperson on some aspect of his or her work. Your goal is to relieve the tension so the interview has the best possible chance to cause change for the better.
2. Review the Position Results Description to set the stage for your comments.

3. Review the goals and the commitment agreement. Discuss how the salesperson's results fit into the total picture of the organization.
4. Ask salespeople to evaluate their own performance and work with you to develop a business plan for improvement. It's important here to get their input and their buy-in to the plan. To be effective, the plan must be one the salesperson believes he or she can achieve.
5. Let them know precisely how they can improve. Generalized suggestions have their place, but specific suggestions have the greatest power to cause change.
6. Ask what management can do to help the salesperson perform better and achieve set goals.
7. Ask what changes and improvements in the products and services your company offers would be of greatest help to them. Listen carefully to the answers, remembering that your sales force is the eyes and ears of the organization. Valuable, even priceless, tips can result.
8. Ask them to recount what they will do differently to put them on track to achieve the desired results.
9. End on a positive note: Reaffirm the value of the salesperson. You want each of them to leave the appraisal inspired to be a happy warrior. Emphasize the sweetness of success rather than the fearsome fruits of failure.

SALES CONTESTS AND INCENTIVES

Contests and incentives can be great motivators—or they can have the opposite effect. In administering either one, it's vital to avoid any hint of favoritism.

Contests

In my opinion, contests are ineffective because they pit salespeople against each other, which tends to degrade teamwork. By definition, a contest means one winner, and maybe a few runners-up. Everyone else is a loser. If your goal is to make most of your team feel like losers in order to exalt one or a few of them, contests are for you. Here's why:

Contests typically work for the first few days and the last few days. People get the announcement and they are off running. The frontrunner usually emerges early and the rest of the team backs off, figuring they don't stand a chance against the top performer. Instead, they walk away from the contest saying, "Dwayne's got it in the bag. This is stupid, I'm not going to bother." At the end of the contest a few people who are still in the running may make a last-ditch effort. Unless you have a really good handicap system to level the field for all team members, especially where the territories are not equal, I would dump contests like yesterday's garbage.

It's virtually impossible to have equal territories, equal enough to convince everyone that they really are equal in every factor affecting sales opportunity. As to a handicap system, I have never been able to come up with a good one.

Incentives

Incentive programs have to be well planned. First of all, you must budget the awards. Instead of just one winning prize, you will be responsible for providing prizes for everyone who meets the incentive goal. Also, figure out what behavior you want to modify. For example, I would never offer an incentive to do a part of their basic job description, such as paperwork. Our outside representatives are always challenging us by saying they don't get the best meetings or enough leads, so I work the incentives around them generating their own leads or setting some of their own appointments. With my inside team the aim is to get them to reach the activity goals each day, so the incentives are built around levels of high activity.

Choose the awards, and do research on what will motivate your salespeople. It will be a variety of different things; no single award will motivate everybody. Some people will want the little rewards along the way such as dinners out, gift certificates, small cash SPIFs (special incentive funds), or rounds of golf. Little things will motivate some of your team, but others will be more motivated by the big win at the end of the rainbow, the fancy watch, the trip, the car, whatever it may be. You have to figure out what will work best for your team.

In the past we created incentives like Results Bucks, which could be cashed in for awards like weekend getaways, movie passes, and jewelry. We would give out a certain amount of Results Bucks for different accomplishments, redeemable under certain rules. If you quit, you lost the credits. As a side benefit, a sudden cash-in by someone who was not performing well or who was unhappy gave us fair warning that he or she was planning to leave us.

A number of companies specialize in setting up SPIF programs and managing the salespeople's incentive credits and the catalog of rewards. You will have monthly fees for this type of service and the costs of the rewards payouts. However, programs of this kind can be very effective.

If you do not already subscribe to *Selling Power* magazine, I recommend starting a subscription. Each month's issue will bring you excellent ideas and strategies for selling and managing salespeople. One of the other benefits is that many of the best incentive companies advertise in *Selling Power*, so it becomes easier to evaluate the different options available to you. Check it out at http://www.sellingpower.com.

Review of Building Effective Incentives

Contests pit salespeople against the other salespeople on the team; therefore they tear teamwork down rather than build it up. Incentives pit salespeople against themselves. This enhances team spirit by encouraging rivalry without the rancor of a contest with one winner and lots of losers. With the right incentive program, everyone can feel like a winner.

Motivate your salespeople with an ongoing long-term incentive plan. Input from those you want to motivate is vital here so your ongoing long-term incentive plan actually delivers long-term incentive. The first requirement is to define what you want the plan to achieve, and how much time will elapse before award time is reached. *Long-term* may mean six weeks to some people and six years to others.

Set the goals. Incentives should raise the bar, but not so high that it strikes your team as being unattainable. In this regard, you can't listen to the naysayers, one of whom Tom Hopkins made famous as "Joe Negative behind the doughnuts." Joe Negative never buys into any positive idea. Even before he finds out what the program is, he's convinced it won't work, can't be done, and is probably a rip-off.

Talk to everybody who hits the production goals, not just to your top producers. You want your long-term incentive plan to inspire your entire team, not just the star performers.

Build the budget. Make sure the higher sales resulting from the plan will provide the necessary funds for the payoff. Budget carefully, and be conservative until your long-term incentive plan proves itself.

Shape the program. As you write the program out in detail, try to anticipate every question that may come up during the program's existence. At this stage, with your plan developed in secret, you aren't yet committed to it. But as soon as you bring in a few salespeople to get their input, the word will spread through your sales team, which means you can't scrap it without paying a price in disgruntlement.

Choose the awards. Selecting the most cost-effective rewards for the program is key to its success. You might want to consult with some of your team's spouses.

Track the program. It can be a success only if you know what results were achieved. This means you have to set up a system to monitor performance.

Celebrate the successes. The program's conclusion provides a splendid opportunity to solidify team spirit and company loyalty. Celebrate it by staging an event commensurate with the rewards. Aside from trip and cash rewards, give plaques or parchment certificates suitable for framing. Salespeople whose achievement during the program reached the highest level should all receive exactly the same award so there isn't one winner and several losers. The same would hold true for those who reached a lower level. Every member of your sales team should receive something, even if it's only recognition for having tried his or her best.

Reevaluate the program. After each run-through, reevaluate the program. Did the results justify its cost? If you decide to repeat the program, continue to reevaluate it after every rerun until you're satisfied it can't be improved.

Consider outside help. Planning and implementing the program may consume more of your time and energy than is justified. Consider bringing in outside sources on a consulting basis to handle the program.

WHAT REALLY MOTIVATES
YOUR SALESPEOPLE?

Ultimately, motivation must come from within each person. No leader is ever the single and continuing source of motivation for a person. While the leader's encouragement, support, inspiration, and example will at times motivate followers, the leader's greatest role in motivating is to recognize people for who they are, and to help them find their own way forward by making the best use of their own strengths and abilities. In this way, achievement, development, and recognition will all come quite naturally to the person, and it is these things that are the true fuels of personal motivation.

There have been a number of exhaustive studies done at many levels whereby salespeople and sales managers are independently asked to rank motivating factors as to their importance. Almost every study clearly shows that most sales managers and leaders really do not know what motivates their sales teams. Most leaders assume it is simply more money, yet that is seldom the case.

You can conduct an exercise in your office as well. Take the list of the ten motivating factors on the Employee Motivation Survey shown here. These ten factors have been isolated from several noted polls conducted by various respected institutions. They originate from the work on people's motivation through the need hierarchy theory developed by Abraham Maslow in 1943. According to Maslow, people have five levels of needs: (1) physiological (2) safety (3) social (4) ego, and (5) self-actualizing. Maslow argued that lower-level needs have to be satisfied before fulfillment of the next higher-level need could be used to motivate people.

Create a copy of the survey for everybody in your office. On your personal copy, rank the subjects on the list according to what *you* think is important to your sales team by giving each factor a rank number from 1 to 10, most important being 1, least important 10. Do this without letting anyone see your rankings.

EMPLOYEE MOTIVATION SURVEY

Factor	Rank
Loyalty from the company	_____
Appreciation	_____
Feeling in on things	_____
Help with personal problems	_____
Good pay/compensation plan	_____
Promotions	_____
Good working conditions	_____
Tactful discipline	_____
Interesting work	_____
Job security	_____

At your next scheduled meeting, hand a blank copy of this list to each of your employees and have them fill it out. Collect the answers and compare your answers to theirs. If they are similar, then you have a pretty healthy environment. If not, some of your environmental issues need work.

I recommend giving this survey on an annual or biannual basis because the answers will change. When we first conducted the survey, good working conditions scored higher than we expected, much higher than the national survey. Since we have a nice office in Scottsdale, we were surprised. When we pursued this further we learned the inside team was very uncomfortable in their chairs, and they didn't like the headsets they were using. So we invested in more comfortable, ergonomic chairs and better quality headsets. When we repeated the survey six months later, guess where good working environment ranked? Down at 7 or 8. The point is, survey results may not always reflect their true motivating factor, but may reflect an area of deficiency.

If you do this at your next meeting, and good pay ranks as number one, it doesn't mean you have a bunch of greedy, money-hungry salespeople; it may mean there is a deficiency, or perceived deficiency, in the compensation plan or in their ability to maximize the plan. Possibly they just don't understand it clearly. Further investigation is sometimes needed after this exercise, but it will certainly give you a place to work from and a goal to head for. As a benchmark for comparison, here are the item rankings based on a national survey that was conducted by K. A. Kovach in 1987, which has been used as a baseline for many other researchers. This will be helpful, as it will allow you to compare how your team responded to how the sales forces in the successful companies of the national survey ranked these motivational factors:

1. Interesting work
2. Appreciation
3. Feeling in on things
4. Job security
5. Good pay
6. Promotions
7. Good working conditions
8. Loyalty from the company
9. Help with personal problems
10. Tactful discipline

Notice that the top three items on the list do not require any capital. Remember when we spoke of the concept of volunteering to manage a group of volunteers. Think about it: If you were going to manage a group of volunteers, if you wanted to create a motivated environment, what would you want to create? That's right, an interesting place to work, a place where people feel appreciated, and very open lines of communication so people felt in on things.

SUMMARY

The salesperson personality is unique. Managing salespeople effectively requires motivating and counseling them on a far more elevated level than ordinary employees need. A powerful way to meet this sales management challenge is to create a highly motivated work environment.

To help a strong performer to get past a slump, the soft approach is most likely to succeed. Question the salesperson as to where you have failed, rather than making intrusive demands to know what's wrong with him or her.

Lead from the front with respect-building attention to your team's concerns. Driving from the rear with the whip of intimidation probably never worked well; today it makes building and retaining a strong sales team virtually impossible.

Review the Eight Steps to a Motivated Sales Organization frequently to make sure you're hitting on all eight cylinders of superior sales performance.

Develop a comprehensive and smoothly functioning system for regular review and performance appraisal of your entire sales team. As part of your preparation for this function, review the Nine-Point Checklist for Gaining Maximum Results from Performance Appraisals.

Twice a year, survey your team to discover what motivates them now.

7 HANDLING TERMINATIONS EASIER AND BETTER

What is the toughest part of sales management? Sometimes it is when you have to let a nonperforming sales representative go. I remember Tom Hopkins teaching me to not call it "firing" someone but rather giving the person a "career adjustment." I'm for taking this attitude, but many times calling a termination something different won't make it any easier. Having years of experience won't necessarily make it any easier either. I remember having to let one of my salespeople go. He happened to be about six feet two and weighed 280 pounds. He was so angry he reached across the table and pinned me against the wall.

I learned from that experience. Now if I were to find myself in the same position I would conduct the termination in an airport lounge. I'd want to know there would be plenty of people around as well as a security force if I needed it.

Most managers I have worked with have different kinds of challenges with letting a salesperson go. Sometimes it's guilt or regret at losing a familiar friend. Other times they worry about not being able to replace the dismissed salesperson with someone better and about the lost sales revenue in the interim. Mostly, I find they worry about making the right decision. Did I act too quickly? Did I wait too long? What are the other salespeople thinking? Did I do everything I could to save the person for the company? Was it my fault it did not work? What could I have done differently?

These are not bad questions. Peter Drucker, the famous management consultant, wrote, "The mark of a good manager is knowing whom to work with. The mark of a great manager is knowing when to say goodbye.

If a salesperson is not performing in accordance with your expectations, it is time for a change, one way or another. One of my favorite sayings is, "If a sales manager cannot change his people, he will have to change his people!"

WHEN IT'S TIME TO LET GO . . .

Anybody can tailspin into a down cycle. Proven performers may need and deserve time to recover from one of life's blows—blows that so often seem to strike at the same time. This, however, is a separate issue from the new salesperson who—for whatever reasons—is not meeting expectations.

With new and unproven people, there has to be a period after which it is obvious that a particular representative is not going to make it. I usually know within sixty days whether a salesperson has what it takes to be successful in our company. Many managers I have spoken with can tell the same thing. They know within a specific period of time whether someone has the right stuff. The challenge we all face is to act on that knowledge and instinct. I routinely find myself hanging on to someone for well over 90, 120, or 180 days beyond a reasonable time limit.

I also strongly believe that salespeople should never, ever be surprised by being terminated. If they are, then shame on management. Salespeople are responsible for, and paid for, bringing in revenue. The numbers are usually obvious and in a well-run company, they should realize as quickly as management does that they need to move on.

Unfortunately, that does not solve the manager's problem. The manager still needs to make and impose the tough decision. A human element is involved; the longer the salesperson has been with the company, the harder it is to terminate. I think one way to achieve guilt-free termination is to work backwards from the decision itself. Look at symptoms and cause and have a system in place to take steps from the first day you begin to worry about the person's performance. If you have set up the proper expectations and used the commitment form suggested in Chapter 3, it becomes easier. The salesperson knows what is expected up front; when those expectations are not being met, he or she should expect you to take action, as will the other salespeople on the team.

It usually starts when the salesperson has gone dry for a while and the manager starts to lose confidence. At this point, you and the salesperson in question need to distinguish between (1) a temporary dry period that may strike a usually good producer, perhaps resulting from private emotional upheavals or other outside cause, and (2) a consistent lack of performance. If it's more than a down cycle—a temporary slump—take action fast.

If you are doing regularly scheduled performance reviews, as we recommend, then perhaps the timing will be good to deal with the person's lack of production during this scheduled discussion. If you're not doing regularly scheduled performance reviews, call the salesperson in and be very clear that you are talking about poor performance and what needs to be done to turn things around. You should review activity as well as productivity.

Don't ask how much business the salesperson's going to do, which is difficult to control. Rather gain an agreement of how much time he or she will spend in front of prospects. You should also discuss what training and motivational materials can be used to turn around the slump.

Create an agreement of what needs to be done in a specific period of time (no longer than sixty days) to turn things around. Of course, it is not over yet; you need to follow through and make sure the employee is executing the plan.

This is a real negotiation and without buy-in from the salesperson it will not work. You may as well call it quits right there. If the salesperson does not participate actively in setting the goals, it should send up a warning flare for the manager. It likely means he or she is buying time to set up a new position and perhaps still take your company's draw or salary. You might ask directly how much confidence, on a scale of one to ten, the salesperson has in his or her ability to turn things around. If it is not a seven or better, find a way to cut the person immediately.

Once the agreement is made it simply becomes a point of follow-through on the manager's part. I like the old business adage, "When you are on track you work for yourself; when you're behind you work for me!" Within a week I can tell if they are going to make their numbers. Even with an honest effort, the process can be tough on both parties. Many times salespeople focus on what they are doing wrong instead of what they are doing right. Your coaching efforts need to be focused on getting the person to intensify the positive behaviors you know are necessary to make the turnaround.

Make sure the behaviors you are looking for are stated in objective terms. Only when they demonstrate that they cannot attain the standards you both have agreed upon do you let them go. One challenge many managers face is that they start out with subjective standards like attitude, which is difficult to quantify. This can create performance anxiety on the part of the nonperforming salesperson, which of course is the last thing you want to create. You are trying to change a behavior. You must reinforce their positive efforts. The key is to put the focus on the right activities more than the short-term performance. In fact, working with a troubled representative is very much like working with a brand-new associate. You state performance in calls per day and provide a much more directed environment.

In letting a newer salesperson go, you may have simply realized it was a bad fit in the first place. Perhaps this person was not meant to be in sales and was just biding time until finding something else. It could also be a mismatch of the new hire's beliefs and behaviors and your product or service. Perhaps, as you'll see in the example of Rick at the end of this chapter, the individual just did not line up with the company's mission.

Tougher choices come with having to let a more experienced salesperson go. These people typically have all the answers, but they are not making the sales and don't perform the successful behaviors themselves. If these individuals admit they don't know everything and are struggling, you can work to help them. The hopeless cases often have weak numbers and are unwilling to learn anything. Such people quickly blame external forces for their lack of productivity. Salvaging any of this group is unlikely.

You may also have a "decent peg in the wrong hole." Perhaps you have a good person who is simply incompatible with the market objectives you have set. Most companies have four areas in which they work to create market share and sales:

- New products in new markets
- New products in existing markets
- Existing products in new markets
- Existing products in existing markets

If you have salespeople who are trying hard but can't meet the performance objective, perhaps you can redeploy them into an easier slot. Clearly it's easier to sell existing products in existing markets, though the opportunity may not be as great.

WHAT IF IT'S JUST A PLATEAU?

Another common challenge arises when formerly aggressive sales-people become too comfortable. They don't necessarily fall apart; they just hit a plateau because they have stopped doing the things that got them to the top in the first place. Your solution here may not be to try to remotivate or terminate them, but rather to take part of their territory and spin it off to a new representative. Although this has inherent risks, it can be effective in achieving the overall goal. My partner, Tom Kauffman, has studied top producers for years and has developed the "Plateau Principle."

"In any organization (business, sports, etc.) individuals may ultimately reach a high level of achievement in which they can rise no further, and thus they have reached their plateau. Unless these individuals leave their current environment (company, team, etc.) and find another organization in which to demonstrate their abilities and utilize their skills . . . they will soon diminish in performance and attitude."

—Thomas Kauffman

How do you know which challenge you face? The best way to anticipate challenges is to go back to Management 101. We have talked about this throughout the book. Get out in the field with your team! If you are not in the field, you are just getting revenue feedback. You don't know why sales are down; you just know they are down.

THE ROOT CAUSES OF PLATEAU

- A real need on the individual's part for something fresh and new.
- Challenges with management have strained the relationship to the point where severing employment is imminent.
- The individuals believe their current opportunity is not attractive or is less than they deserve based on their perceptions of their own value.
- The individuals have been promoted to a higher level of responsibility where they find themselves incapable of consistently performing at their previous levels of success. The resulting frustration can serve as a catalyst for any of the above three factors.

HOW TO PREVENT PLATEAU

- Provide opportunities for employees to try new lateral roles within the organization.
- Cultivate an atmosphere of respect that allows employees to understand their roles and management's role within the organization.
- Keep employees' perceptions in line with reality. (Like it or not, reality is whatever management's perception of it is).
- Don't give away opportunities and autonomy—make employees earn them over appropriate periods of time no shortcuts.

Most managers still manage largely by quotas; they don't manage behaviors, which can be misleading. Salespeople cannot always control whether prospects will dig into their pockets, but they can always control their own behaviors and activities. After a difficult meeting with a slumping salesperson, the manager should monitor exactly the numbers they might have to enforce. If a salesperson is behind by fifty calls or twenty appointments, their sales production will ultimately decline further.

WHEN YOU HAVE NO OTHER CHOICE: UNETHICAL BEHAVIOR

Other than lack of performance, there are other reasons why managers must terminate salespeople. A salesperson who commits an unethical or illegal act such as stealing from the company or a client must be let go immediately. I have had to let several people go over the years for theft. Some of those people I had thought were my friends, and this made it even more difficult.

I also believe you must terminate if you find someone using illegal drugs, driving company vehicles while impaired or—equally dangerous from the standpoint of company liability—driving their own vehicle on company business while impaired.

Others know about this kind of behavior, and it sets the wrong example if you allow it to exist. Such tolerance tells the rest of the team that your moral standards are negotiable. When forced to let someone go for any of these causes, I make an example of it publicly with the team. I do not allow the person who committed the act to quietly leave. Everyone needs to know where we stand on these matters. We have a no-tolerance policy, and behavior like that is not acceptable.

Termination is not a subject we like to talk about. I don't enjoy this task, ever. Few do. However, there are some important facts you should know:

- In 1978, there were only 200 pending wrongful-termination suits in the United States.
- In 1988, there were 25,000 pending wrongful-termination suits.
- In 1998, there were more than 100,000 pending wrongful-termination suits.
- In 2004, more than 250,000 pending wrongful-termination suits clogged U.S. courts.

In a litigious society such as ours, you must be educated in termination policies. If you have ever been through a wrongful-termination suit, you know what I am talking about.

There are two ways to learn things: the easy way or the hard way. You can learn from other people's experience, or you can learn the same lessons via your own experience in the school of hard knocks. I assure you that termination and termination suits are an area where you want to learn from other people.

Let me give you a bit of my own experience in my own company. We terminated an employee, feeling fully justified in doing so. He felt differently and filed suit. When the courts see these cases, do they look with more favor on the little employee or the big corporation?

Basically all the employee has to do is file the action—which can be done without the employee having to put down a dime if an attorney will take the case on contingency—and then the company must prove its case and defend its action. It's ugly. It's expensive. And even when you win, you lose in the financial sense or even in reputation.

Make sure you keep good notes of events, actions, and of any other people involved. Include dates, times, and the reasons for the termination. Get expert help; hire an attorney who specializes in wrongful-termination cases and employment law. Unfortunately, I hired my tax attorney, and he became knowledgeable on the issues, but on my dime. We eventually won the case, but at the cost of $14,000 plus the stress and the lost time.

THE STRATEGIC TERMINATION AND ELEMENTS OF THE EXIT INTERVIEW

No one can know in advance that someone on the team is going to be terminated. You should have two equally strong concerns:

(1) to minimize the terminee's humiliation and (2) to minimize the negative effect on the rest of the team. These two concerns are closely intertwined. Unless terminations are handled in a professional manner—that is, with evident empathy—your actions will be resented by your entire work force. There will be a price to pay for your insensitivity in the form of weakened company loyalty.

It is very unprofessional to confide in someone not in the inner circle of management about your intention to let someone go, or even to permit any discussion of the person's performance. Revealing your intention indirectly is just as bad as coming right out with it. Your confidant can't keep the secret. Persons you intend to terminate will soon hear about it on the grapevine before you approach them, or they may confront you first. You will lose all strategic advantage.

Terminate Prior to a Meeting

I find it better to execute terminations first thing in the morning. Some managers believe it is better to do it at the end of the day. But if I know I am firing someone that afternoon, I stew and stress about it all day long. As a result, sometimes I talk myself out of it or avoid doing it altogether. If I take care of it first thing in the morning, it's done and over with. Then when we meet for a company meeting, I can make the announcement to the rest of the sales staff. While the meeting is being conducted, terminees have time to clear their desks and leave without having to face their peers or endure their questions.

Never Delay Personnel Decisions

First of all, if someone really is not performing, the other team members will start wondering why you are not letting that person go. They will soon start to get disgusted. Negativity will spread around the office and you will lose respect.

Once you make the decision to terminate, do it quickly and never turn back! Never wobble on the fence. Be firm and be clear. One former employee called me after speaking to her boss. She wasn't sure whether she was terminated, was asked to resign, or still had two weeks to get back on track. She didn't know what to do. It's natural to want to soften the blow as much as possible, but this must not be done at the expense of clarity. Leaving the terminated employee confused merely prolongs the agony. Many employees will be in a state of shock when they are terminated, and they don't want to believe what they're hearing, so any ambiguity or indecisiveness is likely to be seized upon.

Have the Final Check and Paperwork Ready

Presenting terminated employees with their final check makes the message very clear and final. It also allows them to know their financial limits immediately, instead of wondering what money is owed to them. They should never have to request their final checks. Imposing this task upon them is completely unprofessional and adds insult to injury. Dan, a friend of mine, had to call his boss about a week and a half after being let go to ask about his final check, which was for several thousand dollars. His former boss said, "Oh, yeah, it's sitting on my desk. I don't know why I have it here. Do you want me to put it in the outgoing mail for you?" Dan was thinking, "Well, duh. It would have been nice if you had done that about a week ago!"

If there is any final paperwork that you need filled out or signed by the employee, have it prepared for their immediate signature or for them to take with them to fill out and send back to your administrative staff, or let them know when any final paperwork will be

182 Managing for Sales Results

sent to them and what to expect. They should not have to call you, or the office, regarding COBRA insurance or 401(k) types of issues.

Bear in mind that most terminated salespeople know they weren't performing, or they know what the other causes for their termination are. In such cases, people often resent *how* a termination is conducted more than the termination itself. Probably a significant proportion of the wrongful-termination lawsuits that are filed spring from the insensitive or unprofessional way in which the deed was done.

Help Them Make the Transition

If the terminated employee has good qualities or skills as a salesperson, and the reason for termination was that the product or environment was just not the right fit, offer a letter of recommendation. If it doesn't violate company policy or your sense of integrity, have it ready at the exit interview.

Stay calm!

The more prepared you are, the more in control you will be. Some salespeople will get very angry or verbally abusive. If you are justified in your reasons for the termination, then you will be able to get through it. Do not raise your voice; do not get defensive. Doing so just adds fuel to the fire if a salesperson decides to file a claim against the company. It is also unprofessional.

Let Them Know It's Not Personal

Express compassion by your manner as well as by your choice of words, bearing in mind that clumsily expressed compassion can easily be perceived as an attack on their dignity. The point is to minimize the damage to their self-esteem. Convey that it is about business and performance, reiterate their strengths (even if you have to search hard for them), and wish them the best.

Give Them the Opportunity to Resign

This is not to protect yourself against unemployment claims; it's more about letting the terminated salesperson save face. When you let them save face, you lessen the chance the terminated person will go away thirsting for revenge. If you allow them the opportunity to resign, then you can go to the team and say, "Bob decided to resign so he could pursue his career goals elsewhere." Everyone will know what really happened, of course, but when your team sees you handle it this way, they will appreciate your sensitivity. You will gain more respect. Most of the time the team knows the person was not pulling his or her weight and they were waiting to see when you'd get around to taking the obvious action.

Have Reasons for Termination in Writing

If they challenge you, and especially if you are nervous about conducting a termination, you will want to have something in writing for reference. This material will allow you to keep a clear head and not get tongue-tied. It will also show the action is final because you have prepared for it. Such evidence of preparation may discourage irate salespeople from filing claims if they know you have documentation regarding the reasons for termination. In this regard, it's often helpful to collect all the weekly logs and other paperwork you can so that you have a thick pile resting on your desk during the termination interview.

Stand Up to Signal the Interview Has Ended

When you are done with the exit interview, ask if they have anything, such as final comments, that they would like placed in their file. When you have their message, if any, stand up to indicate that the meeting is finished. Otherwise, they may linger in hopes you will change your mind, thus making it an even more uncomfortable situation.

MAKING A PRE-EMPTIVE STRIKE

An area often overlooked in creating and implementing a plan for termination is the proactive termination of a salesperson who is not meeting the goal.

This is a method of keeping expenses down. Most of us do not let people go right away; we hold onto them and give them a second shot. However, proactive termination is sometimes a good thing— for the company and for the failed employee. Most of you probably know if a person has got it what it takes within a certain short period of time. In my company, I know within 60 days whether a new hire has what it takes to make it in our business. Get perceptive and listen to your intuition. I have been doing it long enough; I have seen success and failure. Even if I can tell whether someone has it or not, do you think at the end of the 60 days I automatically let the failed person go? No, I tend to keep them between 180 and 220 days because I want to give them every chance to prove themselves. After all, they are nice people or I wouldn't have hired them. I really hate to fire people, but it is an essential duty of a leader.

I learned a good lesson about eight years ago with an employee named Rick. I had to let Rick go, an extra-hard task because he was a really great guy. A member of our inside team, Rick was the kind of guy who would pick up coffee and donuts for everyone in the morning. At lunch, he'd ask if you wanted anything. He was very organized with his paperwork, but Rick couldn't sell beer to sailors just off the ship. He just couldn't close a sale.

Eventually we had to let Rick go. When I sat him down, he cried, he was mad, and I had to stand my ground. I knew the interview would be heavily emotional for both of us, so I was well prepared.

About a week later, Rick called me. "Hey Ron, I was really mad at you last week because I really liked working at Results. But I got a new job this week. It's in the golf industry, and I'm really excited about it. I would never have left your company, because I loved it there, but I wasn't right for your industry. Thank you for the opportunity to move on." I was shocked and amazed. About a year later Rick called again.

He opened with, "Happy anniversary! I met a young woman. She works for the same company, and I'm thinking she's the one. I never would have met her if you hadn't fired me." Cool!

Rick calls me about once a year to give me updates. It's become a friendship in spite of the circumstances of the painful termination. Sometimes you have to let people go because they're just not a good fit and they need to move on to other opportunities. Giving them the push sometimes is what they need most as a human being.

SUMMARY

With adequate preparation, the sometimes essential but always unpleasant task of termination will go easier and better. Here again, preparation makes all the difference.

Ideally, you will accumulate a file on each salesperson beginning at the day of hire. If this is not possible, begin building your file at the first sign of a problem.

Study the phenomenon of plateauing, and how to deal with it.

Never forget the specter of wrongful-termination lawsuits, which are costly in executive time and legal fees even when won.

Disgruntled former employees who know you have thoroughly documented their lack of performance—because they participated in the file building—are less likely to file suit, or to find an attorney willing to take their cases on a contingency basis.

IN CONCLUSION

Your role as a sales manager is probably one of the most difficult tasks in American business today. Managing people in a work environment is difficult enough, and it's even more challenging when you add that most salespeople have fairly large egos, may be independent contractors instead of employees, and often earn more annually than the manager. As I watch professional sports teams function in a world where players' salaries are out of control, I am always amazed at how coaches manage players who probably earn ten times what the coach earns and have humongous egos.

The ideas and checklists we have presented in this book will greatly help you become a better manager of salespeople. It is important, however, to state that there are no "silver bullets" when it comes to managing salespeople. We operate in a very dynamic environment and that will never change. One of my favorite statements is "The only thing permanent about life is change." Follow these principles to the best of your ability. Take time to reflect on the things that work and those that don't. Become a serious student of leadership and you will help others to grow as you grow in the process.

Our country needs great leaders. The future salespeople of tomorrow need you to become a great leader. When you consider the impact of the profession of selling to our economy and the importance of creating professional salespeople, you begin to understand your role as a sales leader. Do you remember your first sales manager? Was it a positive experience or a negative one? I remember very specifically my first sales manager. He was a very charismatic person who was a phenomenal closer. He taught me the importance of learning the craft and challenged me at an early age. I think he helped me to make a lifelong commitment to sales and becoming a great sales leader. I wonder what would have happened if he was like so many managers I hear about who are incompetent leading and teaching. When I entered sales it was not considered an honorable profession; had I been influenced by a poor leader, I might not have stayed in sales. This happens so often, and it is a shame that people that could have great potential leave the business of selling because they were exposed to incompetence in sales management.

Take your craft seriously. Work on recruiting quality people, set the correct expectations, and train them in the proper skill sets. Continue to develop, coach, and motivate your group. If all of that fails, do not delay on personnel decisions. Let them move on to other opportunities as quickly as possible. You have an incredible opportunity to influence so many lives and stimulate the economy in a positive manner. I wish you the best of success, and I invite you to contact me with any comments, to discuss your challenges, or to share your success!

Ron Marks
ronm@resultsseminars.com